Waffles

from morning to midnight

Also by Dorie Greenspan

Sweet Times: Simple Desserts for Every Occasion

Waffles

from morning to midnight

DORIE GREENSPAN

WELDON OWEN
PUBLISHING

Weldon Owen Inc.
814 Montgomery Street
San Francisco, CA 94133

First published in the United States, 1993, by William Morrow and Company Inc.

Library of Congress Cataloging-in-Publication Data is available.
ISBN 1-892374-62-5

First printed 2002
10 9 8 7 6 5 4 3 2 1

Book design by Leslie Pirtle
Cover design by Catherine Jacobes
Cover photograph by Noel Barnhurst

Printed by Edwards Brothers Incorporated, Ann Arbor, Michigan.

For my parents,
who never waffled on their love and support

In memory of Michael Kalil

Acknowledgments

This book was a pleasure to write because of the affection, energy, insight, and extraordinary intelligence of my editor, Maria Guarnaschelli. And thanks are due to Chas Edwards, who is Maria's assistant but I wish he were mine. ❡ It was nurtured by Skip Dye, whose enthusiasm for this book didn't dip from day one; the keen eye of Deborah Weiss Geline, a terrific copyeditor; the production savvy of Karen Lumley; the attention to detail of my agent, Jane Dystel; and the careful recipe testing of Stan Lacher. ❡ And it looks as warm and inviting as waffles themselves because of Judd Pilossof's evocative photographs, propped by Laura Hart with food styled by Mariann Sauvion; and Leslie Pirtle's outstanding design. ❡ I am, as always, especially grateful to my husband, Michael, and son, Joshua, who, in addition to being their usual wonderful selves, further endeared themselves by requesting waffles from morning to midnight—knowing they would have gotten them anyway.

Contents

CHAPTER **1**

Eye-Openers

Waffles for Breakfast

Introduction

Keep That Iron Hot

Waffles from Morning to Midnight has one hundred recipes for waffles and toppings, both sweet and savory. I could have created hundreds more because each waffle idea instantly begot another. It didn't take long before I realized how deliciously without limits the possibilities were for inventing great-tasting waffles. ⸿ Once I tossed aside my outdated notions about waffles being best at breakfast, or suitable for dessert only when serving as a sopper-upper for ice cream, I was free, free to play around with the flavors and combinations that make waffles ideal for midday meals, dinners, savory snacks, and seductive sweets. I was also free to rethink waffles for breakfast—and I did, coming up with such innovative takes on A.M. meals as Carrot Muffins on a Grid (terrific with a spoonful of plain yogurt). ¶ What I discovered in waffles was a food as versatile as pasta, rice, or even bread; as easy to make as the simplest entrée in my repertoire; and more fun to serve—and to savor—than any other party fare around. In fact, I came to think of waffles as "fun food" since whenever I told friends what I'd be serving them, they'd say, "What fun!" And if what I served included waffle chips, there was an immediate increase in the fun factor. ¶ Once you make your first batch of super-crunchy waffle "chips" (waffles crisped to a crunch in a slow oven), the odds are good you may never want to settle for packaged, deep-fried chips again. Why would you, when you can make your own wholesome baked chips in flavors commerce never dreamed of? Try the Cilantro Waffle Chips made with cornmeal and jalapeño peppers and served with Chunky Guacamole, or the sprightly Dill Waffle Chips with a Yogurt Spoon Dip, or, from our own Southwest, Blue Corn Chips with spicy Black Bean Salsa.

These add fun to any get-together, large or small. ❡ The simple technique for transforming waffles into chips and dippers is revolutionary. But the waffle recipes that transform everyday meals into lively entertainment are, in their own ways, just as extraordinary. ❡ Even if you've never cooked before, you can be a waffling hero. Waffle making is not an art, it's a series of foolproof steps. Follow them and you can serve winners like comforting Cinnamon-Raisin Whole-Wheat Waffles or waffled French toast for breakfast; Curried Waffle Club Sandwiches or Sesame Chicken Salad on Scallion Waffles for lunch; Spicy Ricotta Waffles with Grilled Pepper Strips or Mashed Potato Waffles drizzled with Garlic-Rosemary Oil for dinner; and an array of desserts as tempting as Tiramisù Waffles with Espresso Custard Sauce or a stack of Gingerbread Ice-Cream Hearts. And for the kids (and us), there are pleasers like PB & J Waffles, grid-topped waffled Grilled Cheese Sandwiches, and Rocky Road Waffles studded with chocolate chips and mini-marshmallows. ❡ A look at the Contents will show you how appealing it is to waffle your way from meal to meal—and to nibble on waffle snacks and treats in between. So when the maple syrup is returned to the cupboard, keep that waffle iron on the counter. You'll want it ready from morning to midnight.

Equipment for Easy Waffling

Waffle Irons: *Waffle irons come in several price ranges with options that run from nonstick surfaces to sophisticated temperature controls. As with equipment in general, it's wisest to buy the best iron you can afford since a good iron will serve you for many years.*

Each of the wafflers I used had a nonstick surface, something I strongly recommend you look for in a waffle iron—it's a blessing on every count. With nonstick surfaces you don't have to add extra fat to a recipe in the form of grease for the grids, and there's no need to scrub during cleanup. Just let the iron cool and wipe the grids down with a damp paper towel. Nowadays, most of the major producers of wafflers make irons with nonstick surfaces. Irons by such manufacturers as Black & Decker, Oster, Toastmaster, and Vitantonio have easy-to-clean nonstick surfaces.

I created and tested these recipes using three types of wafflers, all made by Vitantonio. Throughout this book you'll find that I give a recipe's yield as, for instance, so many 4½-inch square Belgian waffles, 6½-inch round waffles, or full five-of-hearts waffles. These measurements correspond to the Vitantonio wafflers called Belgian, the one that makes two 4½-inch waffles at a time, each with deep grids; Classic, which turns out a 6½-inch round waffle with medium-deep grids and indentations that divide the waffle into quarters; and Five-of-Hearts, a waffler that produces a scallop-edged waffle that can be broken into five heart shapes, each relatively thin and sporting very shallow grids.

You can make any of the recipes in this book on any style waffle iron, so there's no need to run out and buy an extensive collection of wafflers, although having a variety of shapes and sizes available certainly adds to the fun.

Mixing Bowls: *I like to use nonreactive bowls to mix waffle batter. (Stainless steel, glass, and pottery are nonreactive materials, meaning they will not react with acidic ingredients in the batter.) You'll need three bowls: a very large mixing bowl that can hold all the ingredients in a recipe, a medium-size bowl, and a small bowl for those few recipes in which you'll need to beat egg whites to stiff peaks or toss together ingredients to be added later.*

Measuring Cups and Spoons: *You should have a set of sturdy metal measuring cups (including 1-cup, ½-cup, ⅓-cup, and ¼-cup measures) and spoons (including 1-tablespoon, 1-teaspoon, ½-teaspoon, and ¼-teaspoon measures) for measuring dry ingredients, and at least one glass measuring cup to measure liquid ingredients. I like to have two glass measuring cups on hand: I use a pint measure for melting butter in the microwave and a quart measure for measuring out the liquid needed in a recipe and, often, for mixing the liquid with the eggs and any extracts or flavorings.*

Metal Whisk: *A medium-size metal whisk is the perfect instrument for combining dry ingredients (there's no need to sift the dry ingredients in these recipes) and stirring the liquid ingredients into a batter.*

Rubber Spatulas: *You'll need a medium-size rubber spatula for folding butter and other ingredients into the batter and for scraping bowls, etc. But you'll probably want to have a small spatula on hand, too. The spatulas I prefer are the sturdy ones made for commercial use. You can find these in restaurant supply stores or good housewares shops.*

Hand-Held Mixer or Rotary Beater: *There are often times when a small hand-held electric mixer is just the piece of equipment you need. It can beat out lumps in cottage cheese, blend sticky batters, and quickly whip up a small amount of egg whites without fuss. I use a lightweight, battery-operated mixer that plugs into a charger/storage unit. Of course, you can also use a rotary beater, the kind that used to be called an egg beater.*

Food Processor: *There are not many recipes that call for a food processor, and most of those that do offer alternative methods for achieving the same results. However, if you're like me, you keep your food processor on the counter, ready to go at the push of a button. If you want to use your processor for more of the waffle recipes, you can convert almost all the recipes to a processor method by pulsing the dry ingredients to mix, then turning them out onto a sheet of waxed paper; processing the milk, eggs, and other liquid ingredients together; returning the dry ingredients to the machine and pulsing just to combine; then pulsing in the melted butter.*

Mini-Food Processor: *I find the mini-machines terrific for chopping small quantities of garlic and shallots, pureeing soft vegetables, or mixing sauces. A mini-processor is* *by no means necessary, but if you have one, you'll find many occasions to use it when you make waffles.*

Offset Spatula: *An offset spatula, one angled like a pancake turner, is ideal for spreading batter across a waffler's hot grids. You can also use a wooden spoon for this, but don't use your rubber spatula: It will melt against the grids.*

Cooling Racks: *You should have two or three footed cooling racks—the kind used for cakes. Make sure the feet are high enough to allow the air to circulate around the hot waffles; if they're too low to the ground the waffles will steam and become soggy.*

Microwave Oven: *A microwave oven is not a necessary piece of equipment in the waffle kitchen, but, if you already own one, you'll find it useful for several small jobs. I use the microwave regularly for melting butter and chocolate, heating small amounts of liquid (no more than 1½ cups), and making bacon (cooking bacon in the microwave is a no-mess job). Do not use the microwave oven to reheat waffles; the waffles will toughen and lose their crisp crust.*

A Waffler's Pantry: Stocking Up

Including Tips on Selecting, Storing, Measuring, and Using Ingredients

Baking Powder: *The waffles in this book rely on double-acting baking powder for leavening. As its name implies, double-acting baking powder works in two stages: It starts to bubble when it comes into contact with the liquid in the batter (the bubbles are carbon dioxide and they're what make the batter rise), then the oven's heat starts the second stage of leavening. Baking powder can lose its oomph, so make sure to replace opened tins every 6 months.*

Baking Soda: *Baking soda (bicarbonate of soda) is a component of baking powder but, even when you're using baking powder, you need to add a small, separate amount of baking soda to the batter when you're using acidic ingredients such as yogurt, buttermilk, or sour cream.*

Butter: *I use Grade AA unsalted butter in these recipes. Butter should be kept refrigerated until needed, but it can also be frozen for 6 months. In recipes calling for melted butter, remove the butter from the freezer, cut off the amount you need with a heavy knife, rewrap the remainder of the stick, and return it to the freezer. While most sticks of butter come with tablespoon measurements marked off on the wrappers, it's helpful to know that one 4-ounce stick of butter equals ½ cup or 8 tablespoons.*

Buttermilk: *Buttermilk has a tart, pleasantly sour taste that is a wonderful addition to waffle batters. Most buttermilks on the market today are made from either low-fat or skim milk. If you cannot find buttermilk in the dairy section of your supermarket, you can substitute a mixture of ⅔ cup plain yogurt (use low- or nonfat yogurt) thinned with ⅓ cup milk for every 1 cup of buttermilk called for in a recipe. You may also be able to find powdered buttermilk in your supermarket (it's usually on the baking supplies shelves). Follow the directions on the back of the package. If you don't use buttermilk often or will not be making several batches of waffles, powdered buttermilk, which keeps for a long time unopened in the cupboard or, once opened, in the refrigerator, is a good choice for you.*

Chicken Broth: *Chicken broth is a flavorful alternative to milk in many recipes for savory waffles. While homemade broth is the hands-down favorite anytime, you can use canned broth with success. Whether using homemade or canned broth, it would be ideal if you could chill the broth long enough to skim off the fat that rises to the surface, but this is usually impractical. When I use canned broth, I try to pour it from the can very slowly so I can stop when I come to the fatty part, which usually pours out last.*

Chocolate: *Always use the very best quality chocolate you can find, which means using only real chocolate. Stay away from anything that says chocolate-flavored, a designation often found on chocolate chips. The exception is white chocolate. Since white chocolate is not really chocolate but a mixture of cocoa butter, milk solids, sugar, and flavoring, there is no "real" white chocolate.*

I recommend you melt chocolate one of two ways: either in a double boiler or in a microwave. When you melt chocolate in a double boiler, break the chocolate into roughly even-sized pieces and put them in the top of the double boiler set over hot, not boiling, water. Don't allow the water to touch the bottom of the pot holding the chocolate. Melt the chocolate slowly, stirring occasionally.

I always melt white and milk chocolates in a double boiler because I find these types of chocolate fussy—they burn easily and need to be watched closely.

If you decide to melt chocolate in a microwave (which is what I do most frequently), cut the chocolate into small, roughly even-sized pieces, place in a microwave-safe bowl or measuring cup, cover tightly with plastic wrap, and microwave on medium power until melted. Start with 1 minute, then continue heating, checking at 30-second intervals. Often chocolate melted in a microwave keeps its shape; press a spoon against the chocolate to see if it is thoroughly melted.

Whichever method you choose, never allow water or steam to get into the chocolate. One drop is enough to cause the chocolate to "seize," in which case it tightens and becomes hard and lumpy. (You can rescue seized chocolate by adding a little solid white vegetable shortening, but this isn't really desirable. Better to keep an eye on the chocolate during the melting process.)

Chocolate should be kept in a cool dry cupboard. If your chocolate changes color due to a change in temperature, you can still use it. The discoloration is unattractive but it does not affect the taste.

Cocoa: *These recipes will be fine with any unsweetened cocoa powder you choose; however, I prefer Dutch-processed cocoa. I find it darker and milder than cocoa that is not Dutched, or treated with alkali.*

Coconut: *You'll find a few recipes that call for dried, shredded coconut. If you can purchase unsweetened coconut in a health food store or your supermarket, this is the preferred product. Dried coconut will keep for 6 months wrapped airtight in your freezer.*

Cornmeal: *Cornmeal is a terrific addition to waffles; it provides a sweet flavor, sturdy texture, and some crunch. For extra flavor, texture, and crunch, search out a coarse, stone-ground cornmeal. Cornmeal is best stored in the refrigerator or freezer if you won't be using the full quantity quickly.*

Dried Fruit: *Raisins, currants, cherries, or any other dried fruits should be plump, moist, and soft before they're added to a batter. If they're not soft to begin with, they won't get softer when they're baked (in fact, they'll just ruin whatever you're making). If the fruits are soft enough to eat, they're soft enough to use in a recipe. If they're not soft and moist, you can "plump" them quickly and easily by covering them with boiling water, allowing them to soak for a minute, then draining them and drying them well between paper towels.*

Dried Spices and Herbs: *Dried spices and herbs should be stored in a cool dark cupboard and checked for freshness now and then. If the fragrance is gone, so is the flavor. When substituting dried spices or herbs for fresh, use half as much. (For example, if a recipe calls for 1 teaspoon fresh thyme leaves, substitute ½ teaspoon dried.) When the herb you're using is a dried leaf (such as oregano, thyme, marjoram, herbes de Provence, etc.), crush the leaves between your fingers to bring out their aroma before adding them to the batter.*

Eggs: *All of these recipes were tested with large eggs.*

Extracts: *No matter what flavor extract you're using, always choose one that is labeled "pure"; imitation extracts won't give you a true flavor. Store extracts in a cool dark cupboard and check them frequently. If they've lost their rich fragrance, they will have lost their flavor, too.*

Flour: *Most recipes in this book are made with all-purpose flour, although you will find some batters that need whole-wheat flour (available in most supermarkets), masa harina (found in the Spanish-foods section or cereal aisle of most supermarkets), pasta flour (or semolina flour, another supermarket item), or brown rice and buckwheat flours (found most often in health food stores). If you don't use flour frequently, it's best to store it, wrapped airtight, in the refrigerator or freezer. Before measuring flour, stir it once or twice. To measure, dip your measuring cup into the container holding the flour and fill the cup to overflowing—don't pack the flour down—then take the flat side of a knife and sweep it across the measuring cup, leveling the flour to the rim of the cup but, again, not pressing down on the contents.*

Ginger: *A few recipes call for fresh ginger, a plump root with nooks and crannies. Always choose roots that are firm and full, with a shiny, smooth skin. Avoid ginger with a puckered peel. Most often, ginger is peeled before use, a job best done with a small sharp knife. Fresh ginger can be chopped with a large chef's knife or in a food processor (a great job for a mini-processor). When using a food processor to chop ginger, drop small pieces of peeled ginger through the feed tube while the motor is running.*

Heavy Cream: *For these recipes, heavy cream and whipping cream can be used interchangeably. If you can find cream that is* not *ultrapasturized, grab it—you'll appreciate its fuller flavor and finer consistency.*

To whip cream, it's best to chill the cream, mixing bowl, and beaters beforehand. If you want to flavor the cream by adding vanilla extract or a spoonful of liqueur, you can pour them into the bowl with the cream before you start whipping. You can add sweetening—confectioners' or granulated sugar—at this time too. Start whipping the cream on low speed, then move up to medium or high. To avoid overwhipping, stop beating the cream just before you reach the consistency you want; finish the cream by beating with a whisk.

If you're serving whipped cream as a waffle topping, it is best to whip the cream only until it is what the French call Chantilly, *thickened just enough for the beaters to leave tracks.*

Herbs: *Fresh herbs add enticing flavors to waffles, and several herbs are called for throughout this book. When shopping for fresh herbs, look for brightly colored, unblemished, unwilted leaves with a strong fragrance (rub a leaf between your fingers to release the aroma). I find that herbs can be kept under refrigeration for 3 to 5 days if the bottoms of their stems are wrapped in a damp paper towel and the entire bouquet is placed in a plastic bag and sealed. Wash and dry herbs just before using. When the directions call for snipped herbs (dill is the herb most commonly snipped), it means that you should cut the herb into very small pieces using scissors. To mince herbs, bunch the leaves together and cut with a large, heavy chef's knife.*

Maple Syrup: *Always use pure maple syrup, Grade A or Grade B. Imitation syrups, often called pancake syrups, are overly sweet and taste blatantly artificial. Maple syrup will keep almost indefinitely on the pantry shelf or in the refrigerator. If, under refrigeration, it clouds or crystallizes, just heat it by placing the opened container in a pot of barely simmering water. (Never do this with the top closed.) This is also the way to heat maple syrup—whether or not it's crystallized—when you want to use it as a topping over hot waffles.*

Milk: *These recipes were tested with whole milk; however, they will work with low-fat, nonfat, or even skim milk. Obviously, they won't be as rich, but they'll still be delicious.*

Nuts: *Always taste a nut from the batch you're about to use since the same oils that make nuts so delicious can go rancid and make them inedible. It's wisest to store nuts in the freezer in airtight containers or plastic bags; they'll keep for 6 months. There's no need to defrost nuts before using them.*

Oats: *Oats give a pleasantly chewy texture and added sweetness to waffle batters. The oats used in these recipes are old-fashioned,* not *instant. (They are sometimes referred to as rolled oats.) Old-fashioned oats can be found in the cereal aisle of the supermarket. Use them straight from the box; there's no need to cook them beforehand.*

Oils: *Oil is often used as the fat in these waffle recipes. Always make certain your oil is fresh before folding it into the batter. Smell the oil—it should have a clean, pleasant* *aroma. Oils should be stored in a cool dark cupboard or the refrigerator. Refrigerated, oils will cloud, but this does nothing to affect their taste; the clouding will clear as the oils come to room temperature. When it comes to olive oil, you'll find several grades on the market from pure olive oil, the least expensive oil, to virgin and extra-virgin (extra-virgin being the most expensive and the oil with the most distinctive flavor). Since intense heat diminishes olive oil's flavor, avoid using extra-virgin oil for high-heat sautéing; use it when you can get the most out of its flavor. While I've suggested which oil to use with each recipe, feel free to make substitutions according to your taste. You can also substitute an oil for melted butter in any recipe, using an equal amount of oil for butter.*

Sugar: *Granulated sugar is the sugar used most frequently in these recipes, but you'll want to have brown and confectioners' (sometimes called 10X-powdered) sugar in your cupboard as well. When a recipe calls for sugar, it refers to granulated sugar. Brown sugar comes as both light and dark, and while each recipe specifies the sugar you'll need, you can, if you need to, use light and dark brown sugars interchangeably. Check your brown sugar before using it to make certain it's moist and lump-free (if it's not, don't use it—baking won't improve it). The best way to keep brown sugar moist is to store it in airtight plastic bags.*

Granulated sugar is measured by dipping the measuring cup into the canister, filling it to overflowing, and leveling it with the flat of a knife; confectioners' sugar should be sieved or sifted, then gently spooned into the measuring cup (if you're using only a spoonful or two, you needn't sift; just make certain there are no lumps); and brown sugar should always be firmly packed into the measuring cup or spoon by pressing the sugar into the cup or spoon with your fingers, always making sure there are no lumps (discard the lumps—they won't dissolve in the batter).

Vegetable Oil Spray: *If your waffle iron's grids need to be greased before use, you might want to use a vegetable oil spray. A spray is a quick, clean way to cover the grid's surface lightly and evenly. Most supermarkets carry inexpensive generic brands that work well.*

Yogurt: *Unflavored or plain yogurt produces a tender waffle with wonderful tang. When a recipe calls for yogurt, you can use whole milk, low-fat, or even nonfat yogurt.*

Zest: *Grated or finely chopped citrus fruit zest is a marvelously flavorful addition to waffle batters. When a recipe calls for zest, it means the thinnest possible top layer of the fruit's peel or rind. To grate the rind, either use a box grater or take the rind off the fruit with a swivel-blade peeler, making sure not to get the white cottony pith, and chop it finely with a large chef's knife.*

Substitutions for Special Diets

Waffles are a forgiving food. Not only will they come out well if your technique is less than perfect, they'll still be delicious if you tinker with the ingredients. In these recipes, I used as little fat, as few eggs, and the least amount of sugar as I could to achieve the tastes and textures I thought best for each waffle. However, if you're following a special diet, you may want to substitute or cut down on certain ingredients. Here's how to do it.

Whole Milk and Milk Products: *Your waffles will be rich if you use whole milk, yogurt, and cottage cheese, but they will still be irresistible if you substitute low-fat, skim, or even nonfat milk, yogurt, or cottage cheese.*

Butter: *Nothing tastes like butter, but if you're watching your diet you can use margarine or you can still get the taste of butter by using 1 tablespoon of unsalted butter and replacing the rest of the butter in the recipe with an equal amount of oil. If you must eliminate the use of butter completely, these recipes can be made with oil. I suggest you use olive oil, canola, or safflower oil in a one-to-one substitution.*

Eggs: *Most of the waffles in this book require 2 eggs. If you cannot eat eggs, replace the eggs with egg substitute; read the directions on the egg-substitute box to determine the equivalent measurements. If it's the yolks you want to eliminate, you can make waffles using just egg whites; the texture will be different, of course (slightly drier and a bit crisper), but not unpleasant. If a recipe calls for 2 eggs and you decide to use only the whites, increase the number to 3 whites. If you are serious about eliminating eggs completely from the waffle recipes, I suggest you play around a bit and find the substitution formula that best matches your taste.*

Salt: *Salt is a flavor enhancer, but it can be eliminated from recipes. The sodium in baking soda, however, cannot be eliminated.*

Sugar: *While I would not suggest you eliminate sugar in a recipe for waffle batter, you can cut down the amount to suit your taste and dietary needs.*

Whenever you make a change in a recipe and are satisfied with it, write it into your book for future reference.

Waffling Ahead

Holding, Storing, Freezing, and Reheating

Waffles are a sensational convenience food: They're quick and easy to make, can be frozen for weeks, and reheated in minutes.

Holding: *If you want to keep finished waffles warm while you make the rest of the batch, preheat your oven to 200°F and, as each waffle is made, put it directly on the oven rack. You can keep waffles warm this way for 20 to 30 minutes.*

Storing: *If you're going to keep waffles for any length of time, from a few hours to a month, make sure they cool on a rack, in a single layer, until they reach room temperature before you pack them for storage. If the waffles need to be kept for just a couple of hours, you can leave them on the cooling racks, covering them loosely with waxed paper or aluminum foil. If you've made them early in the day for that evening, or if you want to keep the waffles overnight, it's best to refrigerate them. Stack the waffles, separating them with squares of waxed paper, and pack them into plastic bags, removing the excess air from the bags before sealing securely. For longer storage, freeze the waffles.*

Waffle chips—waffles that have been "dried" in a slow oven—should be stored as you store crunchy crackers—in a tin with a cover. Waffle chips will keep for about 3 days at room temperature.

Freezing: *Waffles freeze beautifully. Stack the cooled waffles between squares of waxed paper and pack in plastic bags. I find the most effective way to pack for freezer storage is to press as much air out of the bags as possible, then to draw the top of the bag together, holding it tightly around the "neck." To remove the last little bit of air from the bag, either insert a straw into the hole in the neck and draw out the air, or press your lips against the hole and suck out the air. Seal the top securely with a wire twist. Place this bag in another plastic bag and remove the air from this outer bag. Double-bagging will allow you to keep the waffles in the freezer for up to 1 month.*

Reheating: *The best way to reheat waffles is to place them in a single layer directly on the rack of a preheated 350°F oven. If the waffles are frozen, there's no need to defrost them. It will take about 10 minutes for the waffles to heat, but keep an eye on them. Of course, thicker waffles will take a longer time and thin waffles, such as those made in a five-of-hearts waffler, will need less time. Waffles can also be reheated in a toaster oven or even in a toaster (although they sometimes get too crusty in a toaster). The microwave is not a good oven for reheating; waffles can become soggy or tough or both in the microwave. Waffle chips can be recrisped for a few minutes in a 350°F oven; check after 5 minutes.*

A Waffler's Tip Sheet

Little Tricks of the Trade

Read the Instructions That Come with Your Waffle Iron. *Each iron is different, and you should get to know yours. Look for the manufacturer's advice on preheating (no matter what kind of iron you have, you'll have to preheat it since you should never pour batter onto a cold iron), buttering or spraying the grids, determining how much batter to use, and cleaning up.*

If you bought your iron at a garage sale (as many people have), the manufacturer's brochure probably disappeared a while ago. You'll have to learn its quirks by trial and error, but it shouldn't take long. Here's some generic advice: Preheat the iron for about 5 minutes (until a drop of batter sizzles when it hits the grids). If the grids aren't made of a nonstick material, spray them lightly with a vegetable oil spray before pouring out the batter for the first waffle, but don't spray for subsequent waffles unless you hit a sticking problem. Start with about ½ cup of batter, a fairly standard measurement for many irons, spread it evenly over the grids with a metal spatula or wooden spoon, and add more batter if necessary, taking note of the amount you add so you can measure out the same amount for the next waffle. Wipe your waffle iron clean with a damp paper towel when you've completed your waffling.

The Number of Waffles You Get May Differ from Iron to Iron. *Different manufacturers and even different irons from the same manufacturer have different surface areas, so they use a different amount of batter to produce a waffle. In each recipe, I've specified the amount of batter I use for my waffle irons (usually about ½ cup) and the total number of waffles I get from each recipe, but you should pour out the amount needed for your iron and make a note of it and the final yield. As you make waffles often and get to know your iron, measuring out the right amount will become second nature, but until then, it's best to write it all down.*

Some Batters Are Self-spreaders and Others Need a Little Cajoling to Fill the Grids. *The best spreader is a long, narrow-bladed offset spatula, the kind that looks like a slender pancake turner. Pour or scrape the batter onto the center of the iron and then use the spatula to nudge it almost to the edge of the grids.*

If You've Overfilled the Grids, Let the Batter Bake for About 30 Seconds <u>with the</u> <u>Lid Up,</u> *then gently and slowly close the lid. If you've really overdone it, you may be beyond help, but most of the time this little trick will save you some cleanup.*

Don't Peek During the First 2 Minutes of Baking. *If you find that after 2 minutes the lid is hard to lift, be patient. If you force the lid, you might split the waffle.*

Every Waffle Has a Good Side, *usually the side that cooks on the iron's base. But you can make the "bad" or "wrong" side better by turning your waffles. When the bottom is properly browned and set, turn the waffle, top to bottom and front to back (so the side that was closest to the hinge becomes the side closest to the handle). Bake the waffle with the lid open until the underside is fully browned and set.*

Even If There's No More Steam Coming Out of the Machine, the Waffle May Still Need More Cooking Time. *Unless you're using one of the new irons that turns out waffles in 90 seconds, you will probably find that most waffles take almost 5 minutes to cook (by which time the steam may no longer be visible). If the iron's lid doesn't open, the waffles aren't cooked. Once you can open the lid, the best way to know if they're done is to look at them—they should be an appetizing golden brown.*

Most Recipes Can Be Multiplied *directly, meaning you don't have to perform fancy mathematical computations to make waffles for a crowd. However, I don't suggest you do more than triple or at most quadruple any recipe, unless you have two irons you can use simultaneously.*

All Waffles Can Be Frozen and Reheated Without Defrosting. *Waffles are an easy convenience food. Freeze leftovers (or a batch that you want to serve at a later time) in airtight bags, separating the waffles with sheets of waxed paper. Heat them, still frozen, by placing them in a single layer directly on the racks of a preheated 350°F oven; bake for about 10 minutes.*

For a Quicker Cleanup, Put Your Iron on a Sheet of Aluminum Foil or a Heavy-Duty Paper Bag *from the grocery store. No need to fret over messy countertops: Just roll up the foil or the bag and throw it away—or wipe it off and put it in the recycling bin. Not only will this cut a couple of minutes off cleanup time, it will provide an extra bit of insulation between the bottom of your waffle iron (which gets very hot) and your countertop.*

Waffles from Morning to Midnight

1

Eye-Openers

Waffles for Breakfast

Waffles weren't baked first in America, but we Americans made them a breakfast classic, slathering them with butter, drenching them with our own maple syrup, and turning them into a national symbol of well-being and contentment. Across the country, waffles are a ritual worth waking up for—and no one tinkers with rituals without risking the wrath of society. ❡ My editor, Maria Guarnaschelli, repeatedly told me that waffles are sacred cows: Everyone who loves them has don't-you-ever-change-them ideas of what they should be like. I found out how right she was when I suggested to a friend that she make a breakfast of my Carrot Muffins on a Grid, a waffle with all the makings of the popular muffins. She looked at me as though I'd recommended replacing apple pie with a kiwi tart as the national dessert. It was no surprise that she was won over with the first bite, but the experience reminded me again of how profoundly attached we are to familiar foods. ❡ So I created this collection of breakfast waffles with one eye on history and the other on innovation.

The recipes respect the traditions that have grown up around this breakfast icon—but they play with them, too. You'll find old and not-so-old favorites made with cornmeal, buckwheat, or whole-wheat flour, speckled with blueberries, sweetened with maple syrup, or served with sizzling bacon. But you'll also find renegades plumped with zesty dried cherries, raised with yeast for a sour-dough kick, or velvety with cottage cheese and Peach-Honey Pour. ❡ No matter how untraditional the combinations, all the waffles have one important thing in common: They deliver the same comfort and joy we've come to expect from our favorite morning food. ❡ They also deliver convenience. Each waffle can be prepared ahead, frozen, and quickly reheated in the morn-ing. There's no reason to reserve these for weekends and holidays; a freezer full of waffles can make waffles on workdays an everyday treat.

Plain-and-Easy Breakfast Quickies

Say waffles, *and Plain-and-Easy Breakfast Quickies are probably what you imagine. They are light, crisp-crusted, and not too sweet; great with maple syrup, melted butter, or chunky jam; and easy enough to make from scratch on busy mornings.*

2 tablespoons unsalted butter
1 cup all-purpose flour
1 teaspoon double-acting
    baking powder
Pinch of salt
1½ tablespoons sugar

1 cup milk
1 large egg

Melted butter, maple syrup,
    jam, or fruit puree for
    topping

MAKES ABOUT FOUR 6½-INCH ROUND WAFFLES

❶ Preheat your waffle iron. If you want to hold the finished waffles until serving time, preheat your oven to 200°F.

❷ Melt the butter; reserve. In a large bowl, whisk together the flour, baking powder, salt, and sugar. In another bowl, whisk together the milk and egg to blend thoroughly. Pour the liquid ingredients over the dry ingredients and mix with the whisk, stopping when the ingredients are just combined. Stir in the melted butter.

❸ Lightly butter or spray the grids of your iron, if needed. Brush or spray the grids again only if subsequent waffles stick.

❹ Spoon out ½ cup of batter (or the amount recommended by your waffler's manufacturer) onto the hot iron. Using a metal spatula or wooden spoon, smooth the batter to within ¼ inch of the edge. Close the lid and bake until browned and crisp. Serve the waffles immediately, or keep them, in a single layer, on a rack in the preheated oven while you make the rest of the batch.

SERVING: When you're flying off to work or the kids are rushing for school, serve these with plain-and-easy traditional toppings like melted butter or maple syrup. But if you've got more time, match these with slices of fresh fruit, mixed berries, or a few pieces of thick-cut bacon.

Cinnamon-Raisin Whole-Wheat Waffles

These waffles bake to a café-au-lait color, send a cinnamony smell through the house, and, like a fine whole-wheat loaf, are elevated to the exceptional when combined with cream cheese, particularly the Velvet Cream Cheese Spread created especially for them.

PLAN AHEAD: **If you want to serve the Velvet Cream Cheese Spread, make it before you start the waffles. Keep it refrigerated until needed.**

The Waffles

¾ cup plump, moist raisins
4 tablespoons (½ stick) unsalted butter
1 cup all-purpose flour
⅔ cup whole-wheat flour
1 tablespoon double-acting baking powder
¼ teaspoon baking soda
⅛ teaspoon salt

1½ teaspoons ground cinnamon
2 tablespoons firmly packed light brown sugar
2 tablespoons granulated sugar
1¾ cups buttermilk
½ teaspoon pure vanilla extract
2 large eggs

MAKES ABOUT FIVE 6½-INCH ROUND WAFFLES

❶ If your raisins aren't moist and plump, place them in a heatproof bowl and pour boiling water over them. Let the raisins steep for a minute, drain, turn out onto a paper towel, and pat dry. Set aside.

❷ Preheat your waffle iron. If you want to hold the finished waffles until serving time, preheat your oven to 200°F.

❸ Melt the butter; reserve. In a large bowl, whisk together the flours, baking powder, baking soda, salt, and cinnamon until combined. Whisk in both sugars. In another bowl, beat together the buttermilk, vanilla, and eggs with the whisk until well mixed. Pour the liquid ingredients over the dry ingredients and whisk until just combined. Fold the raisins and melted butter into the batter.

❹ Lightly butter or spray the grids of your iron, if needed. Brush or spray the grids again only if subsequent waffles stick.

❺ Spoon out ½ to ⅔ cup of batter (or a little more than your waffler's manufacturer suggests) onto the iron. Use a metal spatula or wooden spoon to spread it almost to the edge of the grids. Close the lid and bake until browned and set. Serve the waffles immediately or keep them, in a single layer, on a rack in the preheated oven while you make the rest of the batch.

Topping: Velvet Cream Cheese Spread

Just a few spoonfuls of heavy cream blended into this smooth cinnamon-speckled spread ensures a luxuriously rich flavor and a texture so velvety soft it stays spreadable even when chilled. Try the spread with Michigan Grids, page 54; Buckwheat Waffles, page 58; or French Toast Waffles, page 56.

3 ounces cream cheese, softened
2 tablespoons heavy cream
1½ teaspoons ground cinnamon

1 teaspoon sugar (or more to taste)

Beat together the cream cheese and heavy cream in a small bowl with a whisk or hand-held mixer. Beat in the cinnamon and sugar. Cover and refrigerate until needed. (The spread keeps for up to 5 days.)

SERVING: Put the waffles on warm plates and "butter" them with the cream cheese spread, pour over maple syrup, or use both. Syrup and spread have different charms: Thick syrup seeps into the waffles while slow-melting spread rests on the surface, smooth and sumptuous.

Carrot Muffins on a Grid

The sweet, spicy flavor, sunny color, and moist, resilient texture of these scrumptious breakfast waffles will remind you of delicious carrot muffins. A mix of grated carrots, shredded coconut, tiny currants, and chopped pecans, these waffles are meant to be eaten hot with warmed maple syrup or honey and a dollop of plain yogurt, but I've watched people polish off pieces of room-temperature leftovers as if they were munching mini-muffins.

¼ cup moist, plump currants
2 carrots, peeled and grated to make about ⅔ cup, lightly packed
⅓ cup pecans, finely chopped
⅓ cup shredded coconut, preferably unsweetened (available in health food stores)
4 tablespoons (½ stick) unsalted butter
1½ cups all-purpose flour

1 tablespoon double-acting baking powder
Pinch of salt
¾ teaspoon ground cinnamon
¼ teaspoon ground ginger
⅓ cup sugar
1½ cups milk
2 large eggs
1 teaspoon pure vanilla extract

Warm maple syrup, honey, or plain yogurt for topping

MAKES ABOUT TEN 4½-INCH SQUARE BELGIAN WAFFLES

❶ If your currants aren't moist and plump, place them in a heatproof bowl and pour boiling water over them. Let them steep for a minute, drain, turn out onto a paper towel, and pat dry. Set aside.

❷ Toss together the grated carrots, pecans, coconut, and currants in a bowl; set aside.

❸ Preheat your waffle iron. If you want to hold the waffles until serving time, preheat your oven to 200°F.

❹ Melt the butter; reserve. In a large bowl, whisk together the flour, baking powder, salt, cinnamon, ginger, and sugar. In another bowl, beat together the milk, eggs, and vanilla with the whisk. Pour the liquid ingredients over the dry ingredients and whisk until just combined. Stir in the carrot mixture and then mix in the melted butter.

❺ Lightly butter or spray the grids of your iron, if needed. Brush or spray the grids again only if subsequent waffles stick.

❻ Spoon out about 1 cup of batter (or whatever amount is recommended by your waffler's manufacturer) onto the grids. Use a metal spatula or wooden spoon to spread the batter almost to the edge. Close the lid and bake until browned and lightly crisped. Carefully turn the waffle over, turning it top to bottom and front to back, and continue to bake 1 minute or so longer. Serve now or keep waffles, in a single layer, on a rack in the preheated oven while you make the rest of the batch. Before measuring out the batter for each new waffle, stir to redistribute the ingredients.

SERVING: Served hot, these are great with warmed maple syrup or honey (just place the bottle of maple syrup or honey, cap off, in a pan of simmering water for about 5 minutes to warm) and a spoonful of plain, unsweetened yogurt. But if you like sweet-salty combinations, try these with a hunk of sharp cheddar cheese. In fact, these make great open-faced grilled cheese sandwiches: Cover the waffles with thinly sliced cheddar and broil until the cheese melts.

Creamy Cottage Cheese Waffles

Just a few minutes on the grids will totally transform the bumpy texture of the cottage cheese into a creamy inner sponge. These waffles have a thin crust and a light, lingering, honey-mellowed tang—the best combination I can think of to top with Peach-Honey Pour.

PLAN AHEAD: If you're going to serve Peach-Honey Pour, prepare it before you start the waffles.

The Waffles

4 tablespoons (½ stick) unsalted butter	½ teaspoon salt
1¾ cups all-purpose flour	1 cup cottage cheese
2 teaspoons double-acting baking powder	1 cup milk
¼ teaspoon baking soda	2 large eggs
	2½ tablespoons honey

MAKES ABOUT SIX 6½-INCH ROUND WAFFLES

❶ Preheat your waffle iron. If you want to hold the finished waffles until serving time, preheat your oven to 200°F.

❷ Melt the butter; reserve. In a medium-size bowl, whisk together the flour, baking powder, baking soda, and salt. In a large bowl, beat together the cottage cheese, milk, eggs, and honey to combine. Don't worry if the curds of the cottage cheese remain. Switch to a rubber spatula and gradually add the dry ingredients to the cottage cheese mixture, stirring only until the dry ingredients are incorporated. Stir in the melted butter.

❸ Lightly butter or spray the grids of your iron, if needed. Brush or spray the grids again only if subsequent waffles stick.

❹ Spoon out ½ cup of batter (or the amount recommended by your waffler's manufacturer) onto the hot iron. Use a metal spatula or wooden spoon to smooth the batter almost to the edge of the grids. Close the lid and bake until browned and crisp. Serve the waffles immediately or keep them, in a single layer, on a rack in the preheated oven while you make the rest of the batch.

Topping: Peach-Honey Pour

Resist the temptation to finish off leftover Pour. You'll be happy to have this later in the day to ladle over ice cream.

2 medium-size ripe peaches
Juice of 1 lemon (or more to taste)

2 tablespoons honey (or more to taste)

Bring 1 quart of water to the boil in a medium-size saucepan. Drop the peaches into the boiling water and keep them submerged for about 10 to 15 seconds. Remove with a slotted spoon and, when cool enough to handle, slip off the skins. Cut the peaches into small pieces and puree until smooth in a blender or food processor along with the lemon juice and honey. Taste the Pour and, if needed, add more lemon juice or honey. (The Pour can be made up to 3 days ahead and refrigerated in a tightly covered container.)

SERVING: Serve one or two waffles to each person and pass the Peach-Honey Pour. You might think about adding some mint to the waffle batter; 2 or 3 tablespoons of finely chopped mint add extra sparkle to the cottage cheese tang.

Crispy Cornmeal Waffles

Cornmeal works magic in waffles: It sweetens and lends whatever it's blended with a warm, golden glow. It also delivers the kind of crisp and crunch that won't wilt under fire. This batter, sweetened with maple syrup and tenderized with buttermilk, is wonderful made with coarse-grained, stone-ground cornmeal. Serious lovers of crisp should try making these in a waffle iron with shallow grids.

PLAN AHEAD: Make the Fresh Orange Segments before you start the waffles. Set aside or refrigerate until needed.

The Waffles

4 tablespoons (½ stick) unsalted butter
1 cup all-purpose flour
1 cup yellow cornmeal, preferably stone ground
2 teaspoons double-acting baking powder

½ teaspoon baking soda
¼ teaspoon salt
2 cups buttermilk
¼ cup pure maple syrup
2 large eggs

Maple syrup for topping

MAKES ABOUT SIX 6½-INCH ROUND WAFFLES

❶ Preheat your waffle iron. If you want to hold the finished waffles until serving time, preheat your oven to 200°F.

❷ Melt the butter; reserve. In a large bowl, whisk together the flour, cornmeal, baking powder, baking soda, and salt. In another bowl, thoroughly combine the buttermilk, maple syrup, and eggs. Pour the liquid ingredients over the dry ingredients and whisk, stopping when the ingredients are just combined. Stir in the melted butter.

❸ Lightly butter or spray the grids of your iron, if needed. Brush or spray the grids again only if subsequent waffles stick.

❹ Spoon out ½ cup of batter (or the amount recommended by your waffler's manufacturer) onto the hot iron. Use a metal spatula or wooden spoon to smooth the batter almost to the edge of the grids. Close the lid and bake until browned and crisp. Serve the waffles immediately or keep them, in a single layer, on a rack in the preheated oven while you make the rest of the batch.

Topping: Fresh Orange Segments

This simple mix of sweetened oranges moistened with their own juice is sensational with Crispy Cornmeal Waffles. You can serve it as the solo topping or offer it along with pure maple syrup.

3 large juicy oranges	2 teaspoons Grand Marnier or
1 to 2 teaspoons sugar	other orange liqueur
(or more to taste)	(optional)

Peel the oranges using a small sharp knife so that you remove the white pith and expose the fruit's juicy pulp as you remove the rind. Working over a nonreactive bowl, cut between each orange segment so that the segment—minus the connecting membrane—drops into the bowl. When you've cut all the segments, squeeze the juice from the remaining membranes into the bowl; discard the membranes. With a spoon, pick out and discard any seeds that may have fallen into the bowl. Stir in the sugar, adjusting to taste, and the Grand Marnier. Cover and set aside.

SERVING: Serve the waffles on warm plates with ample maple syrup. If you've made the Orange Segments, ladle them out with a slotted spoon and top each serving with some. And if you have any waffles left over, consider serving them, reheated, alongside soup and salad at lunchtime.

Banana-Oatmeal Waffles

Banana-Oatmeal Waffles have everything going for them: the sweetness of banana, the nuttiness of oats, and the mildly spicy flavor that comes from blending cinnamon, nutmeg, and brown sugar with tart buttermilk. Think of these fragrant waffles as comfort food—they provide the same kinds of pleasures that puddings do.

4 tablespoons (½ stick)
  unsalted butter
1 cup old-fashioned oats
  (*not* instant)
1 cup all-purpose flour
1 tablespoon double-acting
  baking powder
½ teaspoon baking soda
¼ teaspoon ground cinnamon
Pinch of freshly grated nutmeg

3 tablespoons firmly packed
  brown sugar, dark or light
1½ cups buttermilk
2 large eggs
2 medium-size ripe bananas,
  thinly sliced crosswise

Maple syrup or honey for
  topping

MAKES ABOUT FIVE 6½-INCH ROUND WAFFLES

❶ Preheat your waffle iron. If you want to hold the finished waffles until serving time, preheat your oven to 200°F.

❷ Melt the butter; reserve. In a large bowl, whisk together the oats, flour, baking powder, baking soda, spices, and brown sugar. In another bowl, beat together the buttermilk and eggs with the whisk until well blended. Pour the liquid ingredients over the dry ingredients and whisk until just combined. Mix in the banana slices and melted butter.

❸ Lightly butter or spray the grids of your iron, if needed. Brush or spray the grids again only if subsequent waffles stick.

❹ Spoon out a full ½ to ⅔ cup of batter (or a little more than the amount recommended by your waffler's manufacturer) onto the grids. This batter is thick and lumpy, so push and spread it to the edge of the grids with a metal spatula or wooden spoon. Close the lid and bake until golden and crisp. (It may need a little longer than other waffles because the batter is thick.) Serve the waffles immediately or keep them, in a single layer, on a rack in the preheated oven while you make the rest of the batch. Stir the batter between waffles to redistribute the banana slices.

46

SERVING: You can go classic with these, serving them piping hot with maple syrup, honey, or melted butter, or you can dress them up with a raspberry puree, a strawberry butter (mix 3 tablespoons of softened butter with 2 tablespoons of strawberry preserves), or some whipped cream cheese sprinkled with chopped pecans.

Whole-Grain Sourdough Waffles

This batter acquires its deep flavor from the whole-grain richness of brown rice and wheat flours and its sourdough edge from a long rest in a cool place. If you mix the batter while you're making dinner and leave it on the counter overnight, it will be ready to spoon out onto a sizzling hot iron in the morning. Or, you can mix the batter, let it rise, and then store it in the refrigerator for a day or two. Because the batter doesn't need a warm, draft-free place to rise and can wait for as long as you need it to (although it gets more sour the longer it rises), you can fit these fabulous waffles into your life without a fuss.

½ cup warm water (about 115°F)

2 tablespoons honey

1 packet quick-rising yeast or 1 packet active dry yeast

1 cup all-purpose flour

¾ cup brown rice flour (available in health food stores)

¼ cup whole-wheat flour

1 teaspoon salt

2 cups milk, at room temperature or warmed slightly

5 tablespoons unsalted butter, melted

2 large eggs, beaten

Maple syrup or fruit preserves for topping

MAKES ABOUT EIGHT 6½-INCH ROUND WAFFLES

❶ Start making the batter the night before you want to serve these waffles. Mix together the warm water and honey in a bowl and sprinkle over the packet of yeast. (Look at the back of the yeast packet to find out just how warm the water should be for the brand of yeast you're using.) Stir with a nonmetal spoon and set aside to bubble for 5 minutes. If the yeast doesn't bubble—the sign that it's alive and well—rinse out the bowl and try again with a fresh packet. (Don't forget to check the expiration date on your yeast. If it's past the date, it probably won't give you the rise you need.)

❷ In a large bowl, preferably nonmetallic, whisk together the three flours and salt to combine. Pour in the yeast mixture along with the milk and melted butter and stir with a rubber spatula to blend well. The mixture should be smooth and liquidy. If you've got some lumps you can't remove by pressing them against the sides of the bowl with the rubber spatula, use a hand-held mixer to work them through. Cover the bowl tightly with a piece of tautly stretched plastic wrap and set aside on a counter to rise overnight. If you won't be making waffles the following morning, store the batter in the refrigerator for up to 2 days. Remove it from the refrigerator and bring it to room temperature before continuing.

❸ Preheat your waffle iron. If you want to hold the waffles until serving time, preheat your oven to 200°F.

❹ Lightly butter or spray the grids of your iron, if needed. Brush or spray the grids again only if subsequent waffles stick.

❺ Stir the beaten eggs into the batter. Spoon out ½ cup of batter (or the amount recommended for your iron) onto the grids. Since it is a liquidy batter, it will spread fairly evenly over the grids with just a nudge from a metal spatula or wooden spoon. Close the lid and bake until the waffle is deep brown and the crust sets to a lacy crispness. Serve the waffles immediately or keep them, in a single layer, on a rack in the preheated oven while you make the rest of the batch.

SERVING: Offer these with a pitcher of maple syrup and mugs of hot coffee. You can serve fresh fruit (the Fresh Orange Segments on page 45 would be good with these) or preserves, but don't go overboard—these have plenty of flavor on their own.

Hickory and Maple Waffles

Crisply cooked bacon bits are folded into a batter sweetened with maple syrup for these light, fluffy waffles. Blending maple syrup and hickory-smoked bacon makes these slightly sweet and slightly salty at the same time—a great combination that's made even better with a drizzle more of syrup or a spoonful of honey.

6 slices hickory-flavored bacon
3 tablespoons unsalted butter
1 cup all-purpose flour
¼ cup yellow cornmeal
2 teaspoons double-acting
   baking powder
¼ teaspoon baking soda
Pinch of salt

1¼ cups buttermilk
2 large eggs
2 tablespoons pure maple
   syrup

Maple syrup or honey for
   topping

MAKES ABOUT FOUR 6½-INCH ROUND WAFFLES

❶ The bacon needs to be thoroughly cooked before it can be added to the batter. You can put the strips in a heavy skillet, place the skillet over medium heat, and cook the bacon, turning once, until done on both sides. Or you can cook the bacon quickly (and neatly) in a microwave oven. Line a microwave-safe plate with a triple thickness of paper towels and place the bacon strips on the paper, cover with another sheet of paper toweling, and cook on full power for about 3 minutes. Check the bacon and, if needed, continue to cook, checking every 30 seconds or so, until done. (It probably will take between 4 and 5 minutes in a large oven.) Whether cooking the bacon on stove top or in the microwave, drain it on fresh paper towels to remove the excess fat and, when cool enough to handle, crumble or cut into small pieces.

❷ Preheat your waffle iron. If you want to hold the waffles until serving time, preheat your oven to 200°F.

❸ Melt the butter; reserve. In a large bowl, whisk together the flour, cornmeal, baking powder, baking soda, and salt to combine. In another bowl, beat together the buttermilk, eggs, and maple syrup. Pour the liquid ingredients over the dry ingredients and stir with the whisk until just blended. Stir in the bacon bits and the melted butter.

❹ Lightly butter or spray the grids of your iron, if needed. Brush or spray the grids again only if subsequent waffles stick.

❺ Spoon out a full ½ cup of batter (or the amount recommended by your waffler's manufacturer) onto the hot iron. Use a metal spatula or wooden spoon to spread it evenly over the grids. Close the lid and bake until well browned and set. Serve the waffles immediately or keep them, in a single layer, on a rack in the preheated oven while you make the rest of the batch.

SERVING: Although I think these need nothing more than pure maple syrup or honey, I have friends who add a scoop of cottage cheese and others who put fresh fruit on the plate.

Blueberry-Yogurt Waffles

I associate these with cool summer mornings in Maine because it was there that I first enjoyed waffles made with the small, juicy local berries. The memory of those waffles is one that comes back to me whenever I see the season's first batch of berries on the greengrocer's stands. The season for fresh blueberries is short, but these waffles, with their soft centers and mild yogurt tang, are fabulous with cultivated blueberries from any state and can even be made in winter with frozen or canned berries.

4 tablespoons (½ stick)
   unsalted butter
1¾ cups all-purpose flour
1½ teaspoons double-acting
   baking powder
¼ teaspoon baking soda
⅛ teaspoon ground cinnamon
   (optional)
⅓ cup sugar
1 cup plain yogurt

1 cup milk
2 large eggs
1 teaspoon pure vanilla extract
1 cup fresh blueberries (or use
   unsweetened frozen
   berries—do not thaw—or
   unsweetened canned berries,
   drained and patted dry)

Maple syrup for topping

MAKES ABOUT SIX 6½-INCH ROUND WAFFLES

❶ Preheat your waffle iron. If you want to hold the waffles until serving time, preheat your oven to 200°F.

❷ Melt the butter; reserve. In a large bowl, whisk together the flour, baking powder, baking soda, cinnamon, and sugar. In another bowl, vigorously whisk together the yogurt, milk, eggs, and vanilla. Gradually pour the liquid ingredients over the dry ingredients, whisking until are just combined. Fold in the blueberries and melted butter.

❸ Lightly butter or spray the grids of your iron, if needed. Brush or spray the grids again only if subsequent waffles stick.

❹ Spoon out ½ cup of batter (or the amount recommended by your waffler's manufacturer) onto the hot iron. Smooth the batter almost to the edge of the grids with a metal spatula or wooden spoon. Close the lid and bake until browned and crisp.

Serve the waffles immediately or keep them, in a single layer, on a rack in the pre-heated oven while you make the rest of the batch.

SERVING: I'm a purist when it comes to these. I think they should be served on warm plates with gently warmed maple syrup poured over them.

Michigan Grids

Dried cherries from Michigan, now available in supermarkets and specialty stores across the country, are fast becoming a favored ingredient in both sweet and savory preparations. The fruit is great with chicken and game, a good addition to almost anything made with chocolate, an ideal foil for rich custards, and marvelous in these lightly orange-scented waffles. The batter has a little oatmeal and cottage cheese in it—just enough to give it a nice "chew"—and a subtle blend of vanilla, almond, and orange extracts and zest—unusual combinations that give the waffles layers of flavor and an irresistibly alluring aroma. While these waffles are easy enough to be made often, they're special enough to be made for company.

½ cup packed plump, moist
  dried cherries
Two 3- by 1-inch strips orange
  zest (white pith removed),
  finely diced or chopped
3 tablespoons unsalted butter
1 cup all-purpose flour
⅓ cup old-fashioned oats
  (*not* instant)
1½ teaspoons double-acting
  baking powder
¼ teaspoon baking soda
¼ teaspoon salt
⅛ teaspoon freshly ground
  black pepper

Pinch of cinnamon
3 tablespoons sugar
½ cup cottage cheese
1 large egg
¾ cup milk
¼ teaspoon pure vanilla extract
⅛ teaspoon pure almond
  extract
⅛ teaspoon pure orange
  extract

Melted butter and maple syrup
  for topping

MAKES ABOUT FOUR 6½-INCH ROUND WAFFLES

❶ If the cherries are not moist and plump, place them in a heatproof bowl and pour boiling water over them. Let the cherries steep for a minute, drain, turn out onto a paper towel, and pat dry. Mix them with the orange zest and set aside.

❷ Preheat your waffle iron. If you want to hold the waffles until serving time, preheat your oven to 200°F.

❸ Melt the butter; reserve. In a medium-size bowl, whisk together the flour, oats, baking powder, baking soda, salt, pepper, cinnamon, and sugar. In a large bowl, beat together the cottage cheese and egg until well blended. Don't worry if the batter is lumpy or some curds of cottage cheese remain; it will be fine when it bakes. Gradually add the milk while continuing to beat. Beat in the extracts. Pour the dry ingredients over the cottage cheese mixture and combine with a rubber spatula. Fold in the cherries and zest, and then the melted butter.

❹ Lightly butter or spray the grids of your iron, if needed. Brush or spray the grids again only if subsequent waffles stick.

❺ Spoon out a generous ½ cup of batter (or a little more than your waffler's manufacturer suggests) onto the iron. Use a metal spatula or wooden spoon to spread the batter evenly over the grids. Close the lid and bake until pale golden and set. Serve the waffles immediately or keep them, in a single layer, on a rack in the preheated oven while you make the rest of the batch.

SERVING: I like these on warm plates with nothing more than a little melted butter and pure maple syrup poured over them. But don't let that stop you from pairing them with orange marmalade or cherry conserve, cottage cheese, yogurt, or some smoked meats, wonderful combinations with the sweet-tart cherries.

French Toast Waffles

Once I started waffling seriously it was hard to stop, and after a couple of months of making waffles from morning to midnight the idea of using my waffle iron to make French toast seemed like a natural. And it was, especially since my Belgian waffler turns out two 4½-inch square waffles, the perfect size to accommodate a standard slice of bread, and its nonstick finish is easier to clean than the skillet I'd normally use for French toast. (It was this experiment that led, quite logically, to Grilled Cheese Sandwiches on a Grid, page 91.) Even if your waffle iron isn't as perfectly proportioned, this recipe is easy and fun to make— and the results are even better than those you get when you sauté French toast in butter. The iron browns and crisps the outside of the bread and leaves the interior soft, eggy, and lusciously rich. This recipe makes enough French toast for two, but the recipe can be doubled or tripled.

3 large eggs
¼ cup heavy cream (you can use milk, but of course it won't be as rich)
1 tablespoon sugar
1 teaspoon pure vanilla extract
⅛ teaspoon ground cinnamon (optional)
Pinch of salt
2 teaspoons grated orange zest (optional)

4 slices firm, good-quality challah (or other egg bread, such as brioche), white bread, or Italian bread, cut at least ¼ inch thick, but preferably ½ inch thick

Confectioners' sugar for topping (optional)
Maple syrup for topping

MAKES 4 SLICES OF FRENCH TOAST

❶ Preheat your waffle iron. If you want to hold the French toast until serving time, preheat your oven to 200°F.

❷ Break the eggs into a shallow, oblong nonreactive pan. Beat with a whisk until well blended and foamy. Add the cream, sugar, vanilla, cinnamon, if you are using it, and salt and continue to beat until well mixed. Add the orange peel, if you're using it. Add to the batter as many slices of bread as your waffle iron can accommodate at one time, allowing them to soak up the batter on one side before gently turning them over. (Turn the bread with a broad, flat metal spatula to avoid tearing the pieces; they're very soft when they've been soaked.) Total soaking time is about 5 minutes, but you can leave them a little longer without harm.

❸ Lightly butter or spray the grids of your iron, if needed. Brush or spray the grids again only if subsequent slices of toast stick.

❹ Carefully lift the bread out of the soaking liquid and onto the preheated grids. Close the lid and bake the toast until richly browned and crispy. While the first batch is working, soak the next batch in the batter. When the French toast is almost done, turn it over to get a more evenly golden crust. Serve the toast immediately or keep it, in a single layer, on a baking sheet, covered loosely with foil, in the preheated oven while you make the remaining pieces.

SERVING: Serve two slices of French toast per person on warm plates with a dusting of confectioners' sugar and enough maple syrup to run around the deep grids. For a change, think about serving Velvet Cream Cheese Spread (page 39) along with the maple syrup. Of course, French Toast Waffles can be served with any of the smoked meats, preserves, or fruits you'd serve with sautéed French toast.

Buckwheat Waffles

Buckwheat flour is a dark brown, very fine flour (almost like a pastry flour) with a flavor so singular that just a small amount is enough to lend its earthy taste to a batter. Here oats, wheat germ, brown sugar, and almond extract round out buckwheat's deliciously assertive taste, and buttermilk and grated orange zest add a balancing tang and tartness. These can be made in any kind of waffler and served with maple syrup, but I think they reach their peak when they're made in a deep-grid Belgian waffler and are topped with pats of Orange Marmalade Butter.

PLAN AHEAD: Prepare the Orange Marmalade Butter before you make the waffles. Refrigerate until needed.

The Waffles

3 tablespoons unsalted butter
¾ cup all-purpose flour
⅓ cup old-fashioned oats
  (*not* instant)
¼ cup buckwheat flour
2 tablespoons wheat germ
1 tablespoon double-acting
  baking powder
¼ teaspoon baking soda
¼ teaspoon salt
3 tablespoons firmly packed
  light brown sugar

¼ cup walnuts, finely chopped
Grated zest of 1 orange
1½ cups buttermilk
3 large eggs
¼ teaspoon pure almond
  extract

Maple syrup for topping
  (optional)

MAKES ABOUT TEN 4½-INCH SQUARE BELGIAN WAFFLES

❶ Preheat your waffle iron. If you want to hold the waffles until serving time, preheat your oven to 200°F.

❷ Melt the butter; reserve. In a large bowl, whisk together the all-purpose flour, oats, buckwheat flour, wheat germ, baking powder, baking soda, salt, and brown sugar. Stir in the walnuts and orange zest. In another bowl, beat together the buttermilk, eggs, and almond extract. Pour the liquid ingredients over the dry ingredients and whisk together until combined. Stir in the melted butter.

❸ Lightly butter or spray the grids of your iron, if needed. Brush or spray the grids again only if subsequent waffles stick.

❹ Spoon out about ⅔ cup of batter (or the amount recommended by your waffler's manufacturer) onto the grids. Use a metal spatula or wooden spoon to spread the batter evenly over the iron. Close the lid and bake until the underside of the waffle is browned. Turn the waffle over and brown and crisp the other side. Serve the waffles immediately or keep them, in a single layer, on a rack in the preheated oven while you make the rest of the batch. Stir the batter between waffles since the oats and buckwheat tend to thicken the batter as it stands.

Topping: Orange Marmalade Butter

Flavored butters are easy to make, long-lasting, and delicious. This butter is made with English marmalade, preferably one without corn syrup, but you can use the same proportions and methods to make butters flavored with other jams and preserves.

8 tablespoons (1 stick) unsalted ⎰ ¼ cup orange marmalade
butter, softened ⎱

Beat together the butter and marmalade until well blended or mix in a mini-food processor. When blended, turn the orange butter out onto a piece of plastic wrap and, using the wrap as a guide, roll the butter into a log. Seal the edges of the log with the excess plastic wrap and refrigerate until needed. It can stay in the refrigerator for 1 week or the freezer for 1 month.

SERVING: Serve these stick-to-your-ribs waffles hot with a pat of Orange Marmalade Butter in the center—you'll love the smell of the butter as it melts over the waffle— and pass a pitcher of maple syrup. If you have any Orange Marmalade Butter left over, it's great on Crispy Cornmeal Waffles (page 44) and Michigan Grids (page 54), too.

Buttery Waffle Toast

My friend cookbook author Jim Fobel called one morning to ask if I'd ever tried toast in the waffler. He'd just had some Italian bread straight from the iron and declared it delicious—and rightly so.

The method for making crisp, checkerboard-patterned Buttery Waffle Toast is so simple that it doesn't really require a recipe. Just preheat your waffle iron. (Don't worry about buttering or spraying it because the toast will be buttered.) Melt some butter and, using a pastry brush, brush it on both sides of your favorite bread—this method makes even packaged white bread from the supermarket taste good. Put the bread into the waffler. Depending on the waffler you're using (and the shape of your bread), you may be able to use two or more pieces at a time. Close the lid and "toast" until done. If you adore jams and jellies, you'll love the way the waffled grids give your toast extra pockets to trap them.

2

Brunch and Lunch Specials

Waffles for Late Morning into Afternoon

Too often, the waffle recommended for brunch and lunch is merely the same waffle you ate for breakfast. Here, however, waffles emerge as a bona fide midday meal, completely satisfying our cravings for food that is interesting, filling, and delicious. Each of the waffles in this chapter is hearty enough to be the centerpiece of a meal but companionable enough to share the spotlight on a buffet. All pack a lot of flavor on a forkful. ℊ Since I love salads and have noticed my friends reach for salads when given a choice, I've included many salads-on-waffles in this chapter. In recipes such as Pecan Waffles with Tuna-Apple Salad or Tarragon Waffles with Crab Salad, waffles play the part that bread used to play. They provide a catch-every-last-drop-of-dressing base for tangy salads and bring to the table their own distinctive flavors—flavors like scallion, mustard, and nut—so well matched to their mates that you'll find yourself turning to these and the other waffle recipes time after time. ℊ You'll also find a recipe for a waffle sandwich, a waffle twist on an omelet, and some waffles that, like Zucchini-Cheddar Waffles, have textures so comforting and tastes so subtle they fit into both the breakfast and lunch categories, making them great for brunch. ❡ Like all waffles in this book, these lunch and brunch specials can be made ahead. But if you're having friends over, nothing is more fun than to include waffle making as part of the event. Bring the iron to the table, bake the waffles there, and then serve them hot off the grids—steaming, fragrant, and inviting.

Curried Waffle Club Sandwiches

Soft waffles with a golden curry color provide the "bread" for these sandwiches. The taste is mildly hot from the curry powder, pleasingly tart from the buttermilk, and slightly sweet from the golden raisins and chopped nuts. They provide the perfect partner for a filling of bacon, lettuce, tomato, and turkey and a spread of sweet-and-spicy chutney mayonnaise. Double or triple the recipe—these sandwiches disappear with blinding speed from any buffet table.

PLAN AHEAD: Before you make the waffles, make the Chutney Mayonnaise and refrigerate until needed. Ready the Club Fixings.

The Waffles

2 tablespoons unsalted butter	1 cup buttermilk
1 cup all-purpose flour	¼ cup chicken broth
1½ teaspoons double-acting baking powder	1 large egg
¼ teaspoon baking soda	3 tablespoons golden raisins, chopped, or whole currants
Pinch of salt	2 tablespoons walnuts or pecans, chopped
1 tablespoon Madras curry powder (more or less to taste)	

MAKES ABOUT FOUR 6½-INCH ROUND WAFFLES

❶ Preheat your waffle iron. If you want to hold the finished waffles until serving time, preheat your oven to 200°F.

❷ Melt the butter; reserve. In a large bowl, whisk together the flour, baking powder, baking soda, salt, and curry powder. In another bowl, beat together the buttermilk, broth, and egg with the whisk until well blended. Pour the liquid ingredients over the dry ingredients and whisk until combined. Stir in the raisins and nuts and then the melted butter.

❸ Lightly butter or spray the grids of your iron, if needed. Brush or spray the grids again only if subsequent waffles stick.

continued

❹ Spoon out ½ cup of batter (or the amount your iron's manufacturer recommends) onto the grids. Spread the batter evenly over the grids with a metal spatula or wooden spoon. Close the lid and bake until golden and lightly crisped. Make the sandwiches now or keep the waffles, in a single layer, on a rack in the preheated oven while you make the rest of the batch.

Spread: Chutney Mayonnaise

Mixing chutney with mayonnaise tones down chutney's sharp flavors and makes it ideal for this sandwich. The spread is also excellent with ham, roast beef, and cold chicken.

¼ cup Major Grey chutney (or the chutney of your choice)	Salt and freshly ground black pepper to taste
½ cup mayonnaise	

You can use the chutney straight from the jar, but it's easier to spread if it's chopped in a blender or food processor. You can also chop the chutney with a large knife. Combine the chutney and the mayonnaise. This can be made up to 2 weeks ahead and kept tightly covered in the refrigerator.

Filling: Club Fixings

This is the traditional filling for a club sandwich and, following tradition, I suggest you use a crispy lettuce like iceberg or romaine—it delivers the crunch you expect in a club sandwich.

4 leaves iceberg or romaine lettuce, washed and dried	6 slices white meat turkey
8 slices ripe tomato	6 slices well-cooked bacon, drained

Assemble the filling ingredients before you start on the waffles. You can leave them at room temperature, covered loosely with plastic wrap, while you're making the waffles.

ASSEMBLING THE SANDWICHES: Working with 2 waffles at a time, build a sandwich by placing a lettuce leaf on the less pretty side of a waffle. Spread the lettuce with Chutney Mayonnaise, then arrange 4 slices of tomato on the lettuce, 3 slices of turkey, and 3 slices of bacon, and spread with more Chutney Mayonnaise.

Cover with another lettuce leaf and top with the second waffle, pretty side up. Make the other sandwich the same way.

SERVING: These look most appealing cut into quarters and most authentic stuck with frill-topped toothpicks. Club sandwiches are a fine match to freshly made coleslaw or a refreshing yogurt-cucumber salad and they're as good with a mug of icy beer as they are with a chilled white wine such as a spicy Alsatian Gewürztraminer.

Zucchini-Cheddar Waffles

Years ago I made a zucchini-cheese galette from a Julia Child recipe and recall Julia introducing the dish by saying that grating zucchini renders it sweeter and more subtle than slicing or cubing. Inspired by Julia, I created these full-bodied waffles—guest-worthy, fine food for a casual luncheon party.

⅓ cup extra-virgin olive oil
1 large shallot, peeled and finely chopped
1 large plump garlic clove, peeled and finely chopped
1¼ cups buttermilk
2 large eggs
1¼ cups all-purpose flour
2 teaspoons double-acting baking powder
¼ teaspoon baking soda

¾ teaspoon salt
¼ teaspoon freshly ground black pepper
⅛ teaspoon freshly grated nutmeg
1 small zucchini (about 8 ounces), scrubbed, *not* peeled
¼ pound sharp cheddar cheese

Yogurt or sour cream for topping

MAKES ABOUT FIVE 6½-INCH ROUND WAFFLES

❶ Pour the olive oil into a small heavy skillet and warm over very low heat. Add the shallot and garlic and stir to coat with oil. Heat for 1 minute more, just until you can smell the warming ingredients. Remove the pan from the stove and cool briefly. Meanwhile, whisk together the buttermilk and eggs in a medium-size bowl. Add the contents of the skillet to the buttermilk mixture and whisk vigorously to combine. Reserve.

❷ Preheat your waffle iron. If you want to hold the finished waffles until serving time, preheat your oven to 200°F.

❸ In a large bowl, whisk together the flour, baking powder, baking soda, salt, pepper, and nutmeg. Grate the zucchini and cheddar into the bowl. Mix with a rubber spatula (or your hands) to distribute evenly. Pour the liquid ingredients over the dry ingredients and stir with the spatula until just combined.

❹ Lightly butter or spray the grids of your iron, if needed. Brush or spray the grids again only if subsequent waffles stick.

❺ Spoon out ¾ cup of batter (or slightly more than your iron's manufacturer recommends) onto the hot grids. Use a metal spatula or wooden spoon to smooth the batter almost to the edge of the grids. Close the lid and bake until browned and crisp. Serve the waffles immediately or keep them, in a single layer, on a rack in the preheated oven while you make the rest of the batch.

SERVING: Serve these uncut, centered on large plates and topped with yogurt. For brunch, make these part of a larger menu and offer an assortment of smoked fish or meats. And for an easy lunch, just toss a salad as accompaniment.

Scallion Waffles
and Sesame Chicken Salad

This is an adventure in eating I urge all fans of Chinese food to take. If you lived, as I do, on Manhattan's Upper West Side, where someone once jested that judging from the mix of shops along Broadway, the local zoning board must have ruled that every block had to have a grocery store and a Chinese restaurant, you'd look at the ingredient list for this recipe and immediately recognize its inspiration. Chinese scallion pancakes were the idea behind the soft, wildly fragrant, spicy waffles, and sesame noodles prompted the intricately flavored chicken salad with creamy sesame dressing.

You'll taste some of the basic ingredients of Chinese cuisine in this exotic recipe: fresh ginger, Chinese sesame oil, and richly flavored Chinese sesame paste. With the exception of the sesame paste, most of the unusual ingredients in this recipe are available in the Asian foods sections of supermarkets and, fortunately, smooth peanut butter is a fine substitute for the paste. In fact, it's what many Chinese restaurants along Broadway use.

Don't let the long list of ingredients deter you from making these fabulous waffles. There's nothing hard about the recipe, and the results are outstanding.

PLAN AHEAD: Make the Sesame Chicken Salad before the waffles. Set aside or refrigerate until needed.

The Waffles

1 tablespoon peanut oil
2 tablespoons peeled, finely chopped fresh ginger
2 large plump garlic cloves, peeled and minced
1 large shallot, peeled and minced
¼ cup chicken broth
1 teaspoon Chinese chili paste
1 teaspoon Chinese sesame oil
2 tablespoons soy sauce
¼ cup Chinese sesame paste or smooth peanut butter

1 cup all-purpose flour
2 teaspoons double-acting baking powder
¼ teaspoon baking soda
¼ teaspoon salt
1 cup chicken broth
2 large eggs
2 tablespoons peanut oil
3 scallions, white part only, root ends trimmed, cut into thin rounds

MAKES ABOUT FOUR 6½-INCH ROUND WAFFLES

❶ Heat the 1 tablespoon peanut oil in a medium-size skillet over medium-high heat. Add the ginger, garlic, and shallot and cook for 30 seconds. Add the ¼ cup chicken broth and boil for 1 minute. Stir in the chili puree and sesame oil. Remove the skillet from the heat and add the soy sauce and sesame paste, stirring until well combined.

❷ Preheat your waffle iron.

❸ In a large bowl, whisk together the flour, baking powder, baking soda, and salt. Add the 1 cup chicken broth and the eggs to the mixture in the skillet and beat with the whisk until well blended. Pour the contents of the skillet over the dry ingredients and stir until combined. Stir in the 2 tablespoons peanut oil and the scallions.

❹ Lightly butter or spray the grids of your iron, if needed. Brush or spray the grids again only if subsequent waffles stick.

❺ Spoon out ½ cup of batter (or the amount recommended by your iron's manufacturer) onto the grids. The mixture will be quite liquidy, but you should still use a metal spatula or wooden spoon to spread it evenly over the grids. Close the lid and bake until lightly browned and slightly firm; these are not crisp waffles. If you're not going to serve these now, place them, in a single layer, on a cooling rack while you make the rest of the batch. At serving time, reheat for 3 to 5 minutes in a 350°F oven, or use them from the cooling rack—freshly made but at room temperature.

continued

Topping: Sesame Chicken Salad

Here's a brilliant technique for poaching chicken, one found often in Chinese cuisine. It's easy, foolproof, and versatile. For example, if you wanted to make a "French" chicken salad, you could use the poaching technique and, instead of the ginger, scallions, and sesame oil used here, flavor the liquid with a bouquet garni; for an "Italian" dish, you could add parsley, oregano, garlic, and bay leaf to the pot. No matter the flavoring, this technique will always turn out moist, perfectly poached chicken.

1 cup water
½ cup chicken broth
5 black peppercorns
4 quarter-size pieces fresh ginger (there's no need to peel the ginger)
3 scallions, root ends trimmed, split lengthwise, each half cut into 3 pieces
2 large plump garlic cloves, peeled and halved
¼ teaspoon Chinese sesame oil
1 pound boneless, skinless chicken breasts
2 tablespoons Chinese sesame paste or smooth peanut butter

3 tablespoons chicken broth
2 tablespoons soy sauce
1 tablespoon peeled, finely minced fresh ginger
2 teaspoons Japanese rice vinegar
1½ teaspoons Chinese sesame oil
½ teaspoon sugar
¼ teaspoon salt
3 scallions, root ends trimmed, split lengthwise and cut into 1-inch-long lengths

❶ Place the water, the ½ cup chicken broth, peppercorns, ginger, scallions, garlic, the ¼ teaspoon sesame oil, and chicken breasts in a medium-size saucepan. Bring to the boil over medium heat. When the mixture reaches the boil, cover the pot and remove it from the heat. Let rest for at least 1 hour. When the mixture is at room temperature, the chicken is cooked. (You can make this a day ahead. Just cover and refrigerate the chicken in the liquid.) Shred the chicken with your hands (it's the only—and best—way), then set it aside while you make the sauce.

❷ Put the sesame paste in a large bowl. Gradually add the 3 tablespoons chicken broth, whisking until it blends with the paste. Whisk in the soy sauce. Add the rest of the ingredients, one at a time, whisking in each addition until well combined. Add the chicken and toss to blend. (You can make this up to 2 days ahead. Bring to room temperature before using to top the waffles.)

SERVING: Cut each waffle into four pieces. Place a mound of shredded chicken in the center of each plate and surround with waffle quarters. A few sprigs of fresh coriander or some crunchy bean sprouts are a tasty garnish.

I often make a double recipe of the sesame sauce for the chicken, using half of it to dress the chicken and bringing the other half to the table in a bowl so that guests can dip their waffle pieces into it as they eat—the way we dip scallion pancakes at the Chinese restaurant. Also, if you'd like, you can mix some vegetables into the shredded chicken: Neatly diced cucumber and red pepper are good choices, as are lightly cooked green peas, small pieces of steamed broccoli, or snippets of crisp-cooked string beans.

Broccoli–Cottage Cheese Waffles

Golden on the outside, spring green on the inside, this waffle has an unusually tender texture—light, creamy, and appealing—thanks to a base of cottage cheese and broccoli, pureed until sumptuously smooth. The fresh flavors of broccoli, garlic, and scallions are marvelous for midday.

¾ pound broccoli, trimmed
1 cup cottage cheese
1½ cups milk
2 large eggs
2 cups all-purpose flour
1 tablespoon double-acting
   baking powder
¼ teaspoon baking soda
1 teaspoon salt
½ teaspoon freshly ground
   black pepper

4 scallions, white part only,
   ends trimmed and thinly
   sliced
1 to 2 plump garlic cloves
   (according to taste), pressed
¼ cup extra-virgin olive oil

Roasted peppers as
   accompaniment (optional)
Plain yogurt for topping
   (optional)

MAKES ABOUT EIGHT 6½-INCH ROUND WAFFLES

❶ Cook the broccoli until the stalks are tender and can be pierced easily with the point of a knife. Drain and let cool for 10 minutes. Put the cooled broccoli and the cottage cheese in the workbowl of a food processor fitted with a metal blade and process for 90 seconds, scraping down the sides of the bowl as needed. (Don't skimp on the time because it does take this long to fully puree the mixture.) Add the milk and eggs to the workbowl and process for another 30 seconds. Leave the mixture in the workbowl while you continue preparing the waffle batter.

❷ Preheat your waffle iron. If you want to hold the finished waffles until serving time, preheat your oven to 200°F.

❸ In a large bowl, whisk together the flour, baking powder, baking soda, salt, and pepper. Pour the contents of the workbowl over the dry ingredients and whisk only until combined. Stir in the scallions, garlic, and olive oil.

❹ Lightly butter or spray the grids of your iron, if needed. Brush or spray the grids again only if subsequent waffles stick.

❺ Spoon out about ⅔ cup of batter (or the amount recommended by the iron's manufacturer) onto the grids. Use a metal spatula or wooden spoon to spread the batter evenly over the grids. Close the lid and bake until the waffle is golden brown and set. Serve the waffles immediately or keep them, in a single layer, on a rack in the preheated oven while you make the rest of the batch.

SERVING: These are splendid served with roasted red peppers on the side and a spoonful of plain yogurt on top. But if you want to do a little more, you can use the waffle to make an open-faced grilled cheese sandwich. Just top each waffle with a slice of cheese (choose a Gruyère, strong cheddar, or even a smoked mozzarella) and a round of tomato and run it under the broiler until the cheese is melted and bubbling. Add a green salad and you have a company lunch.

Smoked Salmon and Dill Waffles

East Side, West Side, all around the town, Sunday is the time for bagels and lox;
it's a New York ritual. At the risk of being called a heretic, I'm proposing an elegant
alternative: a rich waffle densely laced with smoked salmon (less salty than lox),
fresh dill, and red onion. Topped with cream cheese and chopped scallions or
crowned with crème fraîche and large beads of salmon caviar, this luscious combination
is sophisticated enough to be served with champagne.

4 tablespoons (½ stick)
  unsalted butter
1¾ cups all-purpose flour
2 teaspoons double-acting
  baking powder
1 teaspoon salt
¼ teaspoon freshly ground
  black pepper
2 cups milk
2 large eggs

3 ounces Nova Scotia–style
  smoked salmon
1 medium-size red onion,
  peeled and finely diced
¼ cup snipped fresh dill

Softened cream cheese and
  finely chopped scallions *or*
  crème fraîche (or sour
  cream) and salmon caviar for
  topping

MAKES ABOUT SIX 6½-INCH ROUND WAFFLES

❶ Preheat your waffle iron. If you want to hold the finished waffles until serving time, preheat your oven to 200°F.

❷ Melt the butter; reserve. In a large bowl, whisk together the flour, baking powder, salt, and pepper. In another bowl, whisk together the milk and eggs until well blended. Pour the liquid ingredients over the dry ingredients and whisk gently to combine. Fold in the salmon, onion, dill, and melted butter.

❸ Lightly butter or spray the grids of your iron, if needed. Brush or spray the grids again only if subsequent waffles stick.

❹ Spoon out ½ cup of batter (or the amount recommended by your waffler's manufacturer) onto the hot iron. Spread the batter evenly over the grids with a metal spatula or wooden spoon, stopping right before the edge. Close the lid and bake until golden and crisp. Serve immediately or keep the waffles, in a single layer, on a rack in the preheated oven while you make the rest of the batch.

SERVING: Have fun with these. Serve them with either a scoop of cream cheese and a sprinkling of chopped scallions or a generous spoonful of crème fraîche (or sour cream) and some salmon caviar when you're looking to make a splash.

Western Waffles

Just like Western omelets, a national favorite and a mainstay on diner menus from coast to coast, these waffles are chockablock with chunks of red and green sweet peppers, cubes of onion, and bits of Canadian bacon, all of which soften and meld under the heat of the iron. The result is a satisfying waffle that is lightly browned, slightly crisped, peppery hot, and fit for a casual brunch or weekend lunch. The waffles can be served with ketchup, following the diner tradition, or topped with a piquant tomato sauce seasoned with chili sauce and Tabasco.

PLAN AHEAD: Make the Piquant Tomato Sauce before you make the waffles. Set aside until needed.

The Waffles

4 tablespoons (½ stick) unsalted butter

½ green bell pepper, seeded, deveined, and cut into small dice

½ red bell pepper, seeded, deveined, and cut into small dice

1 small yellow onion, peeled and coarsely chopped

¼ pound chunk Canadian bacon, cut into small cubes

1¾ cups all-purpose flour

1 tablespoon double-acting baking powder

⅛ teaspoon salt

⅛ teaspoon freshly ground black pepper

2 cups milk

2 large eggs

Tabasco to taste

MAKES ABOUT SIX 6½-INCH ROUND WAFFLES

❶ Melt the butter in a medium-size skillet over medium heat. Add the green and red peppers and onion and sauté until the vegetables soften slightly and begin to give up their juices, about 3 to 4 minutes. Add the Canadian bacon and stir to combine. (There's no need to cook the bacon, so don't linger over this step.) Remove from the heat.

❷ Preheat your waffle iron. If you want to hold the finished waffles until serving time, preheat your oven to 200°F.

❸ In a large bowl, whisk together the flour, baking powder, salt, and pepper. In another bowl, whisk together the milk and eggs. Add the Tabasco (making a spicy batter) and beat again. Pour the liquid ingredients over the dry ingredients and stir until just combined. Fold in the vegetable and bacon mixture.

❹ Lightly butter or spray the grids of your iron, if needed. Brush or spray the grids again only if subsequent waffles stick.

❺ Spoon out a full ½ cup of batter (or the amount recommended by your waffler's manufacturer) onto the iron, spreading it evenly over the grids with a metal spatula or wooden spoon. Close the lid and bake until lightly golden and set. Serve the waffles immediately or keep them, in a single layer, on a rack in the preheated oven while you make the rest of the batch. Stir the batter gently between waffles.

Topping: Piquant Tomato Sauce

This simple-to-make tomato sauce gets its zip from chili sauce, Tabasco, and Worcestershire. It's put together in minutes and is the properly sassy partner to Westerns.

1½ cups canned crushed
   tomatoes
¼ cup water
3 tablespoons bottled chili
   sauce

Tabasco and Worcestershire
   sauce to taste

Place the tomatoes, water, and chili sauce in a medium-size saucepan and bring to a boil over medium heat. Lower the heat and simmer for 10 minutes, stirring occasionally. Season with Tabasco and Worcestershire sauce and set aside. (The sauce can be made up to 3 days ahead, covered, and refrigerated.)

SERVING: At serving time, reheat the tomato sauce and adjust the seasonings; it should be spicy. Serve the waffles on warm plates with a spoonful of sauce. If you'd like, garnish each plate with a few slices of fresh tomato or put a large wedge of a hard, sharp-flavored cheese (you might try one that has jalapeño peppers mixed into it) on the table for all to cut into.

Tarragon Waffles with Crab Salad

Crabmeat is an edible luxury, deserving of refined accompaniments—and that's just what these waffles provide. The waffles are flavored with fresh tarragon, onion, and a few teaspoons of dried herbes de Provence—a blend redolent of thyme, marjoram, savory, oregano, and rosemary. Because they are made with olive oil rather than butter, these elegant, light-crusted waffles bake to a pale, almost white color. Topped with a salad of gently spiced crabmeat, these merit a table set with flowers and cloth napkins.

PLAN AHEAD: Make the Crab Salad before you make the waffles. Refrigerate until needed.

The Waffles

1¼ cups all-purpose flour
1½ teaspoons double-acting
   baking powder
1 teaspoon salt
½ teaspoon freshly ground
   black pepper
2 teaspoons herbes de
   Provence
1¼ cups milk
2 large eggs
Dash of Tabasco

2 tablespoons finely chopped
   fresh tarragon
1 small yellow onion, peeled
   and finely chopped
3 tablespoons extra-virgin
   olive oil

Lettuce leaves, tomato slices,
   and chives for garnish
   (optional)

MAKES ABOUT FOUR 6½-INCH ROUND WAFFLES

❶ Preheat your waffle iron. If you want to hold the finished waffles until serving time, preheat your oven to 200°F.

❷ In a large bowl, whisk together the flour, baking powder, salt, pepper, and herbes de Provence. In another bowl, whisk together the milk, eggs, and Tabasco until well blended. Pour the liquid ingredients over the dry ingredients and stir with the whisk until just combined. Stir in the tarragon, onion, and olive oil.

❸ Lightly butter or spray the grids of your iron, if needed. Brush or spray the grids again only if subsequent waffles stick.

❹ Spoon out about ⅔ cup of batter (or the amount your waffler's manufacturer recommends) onto the iron. Spread the batter evenly across the grids with a metal spatula or wooden spoon. Close the lid and bake until the waffle sets. Serve the waffles immediately or keep them, in a single layer, on a rack in the preheated oven while you make the rest of the batch.

Topping: Crab Salad

This is an excellent way to prepare crab salad. The addition of scallions, chives, and lemon juice provides a sharp, spirited counterbalance to crab's sweet, sea-salty flavor. Don't turn your nose up at the ketchup in the mayonnaise dressing; it blends in beautifully with these flavors and does nothing to diminish the salad's delicacy.

1 pound crabmeat, cartilage removed, flaked
6 scallions, white part only, trimmed and thinly sliced
2 tablespoons snipped fresh chives
1½ tablespoons lemon juice (or more to taste)

⅔ cup mayonnaise
2 tablespoons ketchup
Salt and freshly ground black pepper to taste
Tabasco to taste
2 medium tomatoes, seeded, juiced, and finely diced

Put the crabmeat in a large salad bowl and, using a fork, toss it with the scallions, chives, lemon juice, mayonnaise, and ketchup until evenly blended. Season with salt, pepper, and Tabasco and taste for seasonings and lemon juice, adding more if you think they are needed. Cover with plastic wrap and set aside. (You can make this a few hours ahead. Just wrap it well and refrigerate until serving time.) Right before you're ready to serve, stir in the diced tomatoes.

SERVING: There is no reason to dress these up excessively—they're both pretty and delicious served one waffle to a plate with a scoop of Crab Salad in the center. A few simple embellishments can make them even more special: Put a small lettuce leaf in the center of a large plate (a leaf of Boston lettuce makes its own attractive container), fill it with Crab Salad, garnish with tomato wedges, top with snipped chives, and surround with waffle wedges.

Mustard Waffles with Chunky Egg Salad

For millennia the Chinese have known that you can change the taste of a food simply by changing the way it is cut. While cutting hard-boiled eggs into large dice doesn't transform them into exotica, it does make for a different—and delectable—egg salad. And serving this chunky, pepper-speckled salad over spicy mustard-buttermilk waffles certainly sets it apart from all other easy-to-do egg dishes.

PLAN AHEAD: Before you prepare the waffles, make the Chunky Egg Salad and refrigerate it until needed.

The Waffles

3 tablespoons unsalted butter
1 cup all-purpose flour
1½ teaspoons double-acting
   baking powder
¼ teaspoon baking soda
½ teaspoon salt
¼ teaspoon freshly ground
   black pepper
1½ cups buttermilk

1 large egg
⅓ cup Dijon mustard
1 tablespoon snipped fresh
   chives or dill
1 tablespoon minced fresh
   parsley

Arugula or lettuce leaves and
   slices of tomato for
   accompaniment (optional)

MAKES ABOUT FIVE 6½-INCH ROUND WAFFLES

❶ Preheat your waffle iron. If you want to hold the finished waffles until serving time, preheat your oven to 200°F.

❷ Melt the butter; reserve. In a large bowl, whisk together the flour, baking powder, baking soda, salt, and pepper. In another bowl, whisk the buttermilk, egg, and mustard to blend. Pour the liquid ingredients over the dry ingredients and whisk until just combined. Stir in the chives, parsley, and melted butter.

❸ Lightly butter or spray the grids of your iron, if needed. Brush or spray the grids again only if subsequent waffles stick.

❹ Spoon out ½ cup of batter (or the amount your waffler's manufacturer recommends) onto the hot grids. Use a metal spatula or wooden spoon to spread the batter evenly across the grids. Close the lid and bake until the waffle is nicely browned and set. Serve the waffles immediately or keep them, in a single layer, on a rack in the preheated oven while you make the rest of the batch.

Topping: Chunky Egg Salad

I think that folding in small squares of red, yellow, and green bell peppers is one of the prettiest ways to finish this salad, but there are so many other additions that are equally delightful. Experiment with pickle relish, capers (rinsed and patted dry), sliced green and black olives, or slivers of sun-dried tomatoes. The excitement of this salad is its endless variety.

8 hard-boiled eggs, peeled
3 to 4 tablespoons mayonnaise
1 to 2 heaping teaspoons Dijon
   mustard

Salt and freshly ground black
   pepper to taste
⅓ cup finely diced red, green,
   and yellow bell peppers

Slice the eggs in one direction with an egg slicer, then, holding the slices together, reposition the egg in the slicer so that the next cut produces cubes. If you do not have an egg slicer (they're available in housewares shops and most supermarkets), cut the eggs with a knife or, if you prefer, mash the eggs as you would for a traditional egg salad. Put the cubes in a mixing bowl, add the mayonnaise, mustard, salt, and pepper, and stir gently to mix. Taste and adjust the seasonings. Stir in the diced peppers. Cover the salad with plastic wrap and refrigerate until needed. (The egg salad can be made a day ahead, wrapped well, and kept refrigerated.)

SERVING: Place a warm waffle in the center of a luncheon plate. Top with an inner circle of arugula (a bitter green that's a good match to egg salad's sweetness) or lettuce, if you're using it, add a scoop of salad, and, if you'd like, finish with a few slices of tomato. Try this with an iced spiced or herbal tea such as citrus, mint, or rosemary.

Pecan Waffles with Tuna-Apple Salad

Here's an upscale rendition of tuna on toast. The tuna is a chunky salad and the "toast" is a soft, blond waffle studded with sweet pecans.

PLAN AHEAD: You can make the Tuna-Apple Salad up to 2 hours ahead of the waffles; cover and refrigerate until needed.

The Waffles

4 tablespoons (½ stick) unsalted butter

⅓ cup pecans

1¼ cups all-purpose flour

½ cup pecans

2 teaspoons double-acting baking powder

1 teaspoon salt

¼ teaspoon freshly ground black pepper

1⅓ cups milk

2 large eggs

2 tablespoons chopped fresh parsley

2 tablespoons snipped fresh chives

MAKES ABOUT SIX 6½-INCH ROUND WAFFLES

❶ Preheat your waffle iron. If you want to hold the finished waffles until serving time, preheat your oven to 200°F.

❷ Melt the butter; reserve. Put the ⅓ cup pecans into the workbowl of a food processor fitted with a metal blade and pulse several times to finely chop. Turn the chopped nuts out onto a piece of waxed paper and reserve. Put the flour and the ½ cup pecans into the workbowl and pulse several times to mix, then process until the nuts are pulverized. Add the baking powder, salt, and pepper and pulse once or twice to mix. In a bowl, whisk together the milk and eggs. With the motor running, add the egg mixture to the food processor, processing until just blended. Add the melted butter and pulse three times. Add the parsley, chives, and reserved chopped nuts and pulse to mix. You can either pour the batter onto the iron directly from the workbowl (it's liquidy enough to do this) or transfer the batter to a wide-mouthed pitcher or bowl (it's another thing to wash, but it's easy to ladle out the batter this way).

❸ Lightly butter or spray the grids of your iron, if needed. Brush or spray the grids again only if subsequent waffles stick.

❹ Spoon out ½ cup of batter (or the amount recommended by your waffler's manufacturer) onto the iron and spread it gently across the grids with a metal spatula or wooden spoon. Close the lid and bake until very lightly browned and nicely crisped. Serve immediately or keep the finished waffles, in a single layer, on a rack in the preheated oven while you make the rest of the batch. You can enjoy these waffles when they're just slightly warm or even at room temperature, but their flavor is nuttier when they're hot.

Topping: Tuna-Apple Salad

This is my favorite way to make tuna salad. Depending on what's available in the market or what I have on hand, I might add chick-peas, kernel corn, small cubes of cucumber or zucchini, thin slices of fennel, or shreds of snow peas. It's a salad that lends itself to variations.

2 tablespoons Dijon mustard
¼ cup white wine vinegar
1 teaspoon salt (or to taste)
½ teaspoon freshly ground
  black pepper (or to taste)
2 teaspoons honey
⅔ cup extra-virgin olive oil
¼ cup buttermilk
Two 12¼-ounce cans white
  meat tuna, packed in water
  or oil
2 Red Delicious apples, cored
  and cut into small dice
  (do *not* peel)

2 ribs celery, trimmed and cut
  into small dice
1 large red bell pepper, seeded,
  deveined, and cut into small
  dice
6 scallions, white part only,
  trimmed and finely sliced
½ cup plump, moist currants
  (optional)
⅓ cup coarsely chopped pecans
2 tablespoons chopped fresh
  parsley
2 tablespoons snipped fresh
  chives

In a large bowl, whisk together the mustard, vinegar, salt, pepper, and honey. Slowly add the olive oil, whisking all the while, until the dressing is well blended and does not separate. Whisk in the buttermilk. Drain the tuna well and empty it into the bowl, pulling it out of the cans with the tines of a fork—a method that produces large chunks. Add the rest of the ingredients and toss to mix. Taste the salad and add more salt or pepper, if needed.

SERVING: Toss the salad once before serving. Place a waffle in the center of a plate and top with a generous helping of Tuna-Apple Salad. Simplicity itself.

3

Just for Kids

Sweet and Savory Child Pleasers

Many of us cherish waffle memories the way the French writer Marcel Proust recalled his madeleine—one taste of it brought back his entire childhood. One mention was enough to make Susy Davidson, former food editor of *Food & Wine* magazine, smile from ear to ear. She recalled that waffles were a once-a-month treat when she was a kid: "My mother would tell us we were going to have 'breakfast for dinner,' and we knew immediately that meant waffles and syrup. We also knew it meant we had to take a bath and dress for bed. It was the only time we were ever allowed to eat supper in our pajamas, and we loved it." ❡ Susy isn't alone in treasuring memories of waffles. I was astonished by the number of people—high-powered business executives, restaurant critics, professional chefs, grade-schoolers, and college students— who, on hearing the word *waffles,* couldn't wait to tell me a story. ❡ It was this response that inspired me to create a chapter of child pleasers. There are many recipes in the other chapters that will delight children, but these are "just for kids." The waffles feature the flavors of American childhoods: apples, pears, butterscotch, bananas, honey, hot fudge; the foods are grilled cheese, tuna, and peanut butter and jelly; and the textures range from marshmallow soft to chocolate-chip crunchy. There are sweet and savory waffles, and choices for any meal and every snack time.

❡ Have fun with your kids when you make these waffles. They're perfect for waffle irons that bake waffles in the shapes of cartoon characters, but will work with any traditional waffle iron as well. No matter what shape you make them in, they'll be a hit at a birthday party. In fact, you can build a fabulous party around waffles even when it isn't anyone's birthday. While your children and their friends might be too young to make their own waffles (the iron does get very hot), they can help mix the batter and they can certainly help make the toppings. Offer many toppings, including maple syrup, honey, yogurt, jams and jellies, and applesauce. If it's dessert, you can serve ice cream, hot fudge, and whipped cream, too. Let the kids create their own combinations. This is how memories are made.

Grilled Cheese Sandwiches on a Grid

The key to a superior grilled cheese sandwich lies in weighting it down during its cooking, something the waffle iron does naturally. By brushing both sides of the sandwich with melted butter, pressing it into the waffler, and allowing the pressure of the iron to meld the ingredients, you'll produce a sandwich with thin outer layers of crispy, grid-topped toasted bread and a filling of perfectly melted, piping-hot cheese.

2 tablespoons unsalted butter
4 slices white or whole-wheat
   bread, crusts trimmed or
   intact

Mustard, mayonnaise, or butter
4 slices cheese, such as
   cheddar or Swiss
4 slices tomato (optional)

MAKES TWO 4½-INCH SQUARE SANDWICHES IN A BELGIAN
WAFFLER

❶ Preheat your waffle iron. These sandwiches are most easily made in nonstick or well-seasoned wafflers. If you think you might have a problem if cheese oozes out of the sandwich and sticks to your iron (and these sandwiches do have a tendency to ooze), brush the grids with flavorless oil or melted butter, or spray them with a vegetable oil spray before beginning. Melt the butter; reserve for brushing the outside of the sandwiches.

❷ Spread one side of each slice of bread with mustard, mayonnaise, or butter. Place 2 pieces of cheese on each of 2 slices of bread, trimming the cheese if necessary so that it doesn't extend beyond the edges of the bread. Add the tomatoes, if using them, and cover with the remaining slices of bread, mustard side down.

❸ Brush one side of each sandwich with some melted butter and place the sandwiches, butter side down, in the iron. Brush the top side with butter and lower the lid. The lid won't close completely, but that's OK. Hold it down, pressing very gently, and bake for about 2 minutes. Open the lid and carefully lift the sandwiches off the grids, one at time, turning them over and rotating them so that the edge that was closest to the hinge (the edge that is thinnest) is now farthest from the hinge. Close the iron and continue to bake until the cheese is melted and the bread is beautifully golden and crisp. Remove the sandwiches from the iron and serve immediately.

SERVING: Quarter the hot sandwiches and serve with fresh coleslaw, dill pickles, or potato chips.

PB&J Waffles

Peanut butter and jelly is the quintessential American kid food, beloved enough to be known by its initials, PB & J. Normally midday sustenance for schoolchildren, it becomes fit for breakfast, lunch, or an afternoon snack when the crunchy peanut butter is blended into fluffy waffles and the jelly is used to fill the grids. The peanut butter flavor is unmistakable in these lightly browned waffles, but not even a hint of its thick, slow-to-spread quality remains after whipped egg whites are folded into the batter and the waffle iron's heat blends all the ingredients. What's left is peanut butter's hallmark flavor and crunch and an aroma of nuts, browning butter, and warm sugar that will draw both children and adults to the kitchen.

3 tablespoons unsalted butter

1¼ cups all-purpose flour

1 tablespoon double-acting
baking powder

¼ teaspoon baking soda

¼ teaspoon ground cinnamon

3 tablespoons sugar

⅓ cup crunchy peanut butter

2 large eggs, separated

1¼ cups milk

Jelly or jam for topping

MAKES ABOUT FIVE 6½-INCH ROUND WAFFLES OR ABOUT EIGHT
4½-INCH SQUARE BELGIAN WAFFLES

❶ Preheat your waffle iron. If you want to hold the finished waffles until serving time, preheat your oven to 200°F.

❷ Melt the butter; reserve. Whisk together the flour, baking powder, baking soda, cinnamon, and sugar in a medium-size bowl and set aside. In a large bowl, cream the peanut butter and egg yolks together with a rubber spatula until blended. The mixture will be very stiff. Add about ½ cup of the milk and mix it in with the rubber spatula. This can be a bit awkward. Your best bet is to press the mixture against the sides of the bowl to start the blending process, then stir. The mixture will never be smooth, but most of it will blend, and you'll get a lumpy but liquidy mixture. Pour in the rest of the milk and stir with the spatula. Turn all the dry ingredients into the peanut butter mixture and stir with the rubber spatula until just combined. Fold in the melted butter.

❸ In a clean dry bowl, with clean dry beaters, whip the egg whites until they are stiff but not dry. Fold them into the waffle batter with the spatula.

❹ Lightly butter or spray the grids of your iron, if needed. Brush or spray the grids again only if subsequent waffles stick.

❺ Spoon out a generous ½-cup of batter (or a little more than the amount recommended by your waffler's manufacturer) onto the iron. Spread the batter to the edge of the grids with a metal spatula or wooden spoon. Close the lid and bake until the waffle is a deep golden brown. Serve immediately or keep the finished waffles, in a single layer, on a rack in the preheated oven while you make the rest of the batch.

SERVING: The easiest way to serve these waffles is to empty the jar of jelly or jam into a bowl, bring it to the table with a small spoon, and encourage the children to use the jelly to fill the little waffle squares in whatever pattern they choose. These are even more fun for kids if you pour the jelly into a squeeze bottle. And for a party, if you fill the squares ahead of time, you can serve these at room temperature instead of cookies or cake. Just warm the jelly or jam with a spoonful of water in a microwave or in a small saucepan over low heat, letting it boil for a minute. (Boiling the jam will allow it to set when cool.) Fill each waffle square with the jam. Let it cool, and refill those squares in which the waffle has absorbed all the jam. Cut the waffles into small pieces and arrange them on serving platters. You can do these a few hours ahead; the waffles will soften but remain delicious.

Rocky Road Waffles

Rocky road is perhaps best known as a name for ice cream in which the "rocks" along the "road" are chocolate chips, marshmallows, and chopped nuts. As ice cream, the combination is consummately crunchy, but when the same rocks are folded into a waffle batter, the road isn't nearly as bumpy because only the pieces of walnut retain their full measure of crunch. These waffles deliver all the fun of the ice cream that inspired them but taste even more like the ingredients that gave them their name: The dark chocolate chips soften and spread their flavor throughout the waffle and the mini-marshmallows dissolve into the batter, sweeten the waffle, flavor it with vanilla, and make its scrumptious inner sponge even creamier.

PLAN AHEAD: **Make the Hot Fudge Sauce before you start the waffles.**

3 tablespoons unsalted butter
1½ cups all-purpose flour
2 teaspoons double-acting
   baking powder
Dash of salt
⅓ cup sugar
1½ cups milk
2 large eggs
1 teaspoon pure vanilla extract

⅓ cup chocolate chips
   (preferably mini-chips, but
   regular-size chips are OK)
⅓ cup mini-marshmallows
¼ cup coarsely chopped
   walnuts

Ice cream as accompaniment

MAKES ABOUT TEN 4½-INCH SQUARE BELGIAN WAFFLES

❶ Preheat your waffle iron. If you want to hold the finished waffles until serving time, preheat your oven to 200°F.

❷ Melt the butter; reserve. In a large bowl, whisk together the flour, baking powder, salt, and sugar. In another bowl, whisk together the milk, eggs, and vanilla until well blended. Pour the liquid ingredients over the dry ingredients and stir with the whisk until just combined. Fold in the chocolate chips, marshmallows, and walnuts, then the melted butter.

❸ Whether or not your iron's grids are well seasoned or made of a nonstick material, it's best to lightly butter or spray the grids since the marshmallows have a tendency to stick. Brush or spray the grids again only if subsequent waffles stick.

❹ Measure out 1 cup of batter for a Belgian waffle iron (or the amount recommended by your waffler's manufacturer). Scrape it out onto the grids and spread it evenly over the iron with a metal spatula or wooden spoon. Close the lid and bake until browned and crisp. Place finished waffles in a single layer on a cooling rack or keep them on a rack in the preheated oven while you make the rest of the batch.

Topping: Hot Fudge Sauce

This is a rich, glossy, satiny-smooth sauce that won't harden when it touches ice cream. It is minimally sweet and maximally chocolaty, ideal over these Rocky Roads and so many other dessert waffles.

3 ounces high-quality bittersweet chocolate, such as Lindt or Tobler	3 tablespoons light corn syrup
	2 tablespoons sugar
3 tablespoons unsalted butter	Pinch of salt
¼ cup Dutch-processed cocoa	1 tablespoon pure vanilla extract
¾ cup heavy cream	

❶ Melt the chocolate and butter together in the top of a double boiler or in a bowl in a microwave. When the mixture is completely melted, remove from the heat and stir in the cocoa; set aside.

❷ Put the cream, corn syrup, sugar, and salt in a medium-size saucepan and bring to the boil. Don't walk away from the pot: This mixture bubbles up. Remove from the heat and stir in the vanilla and the reserved chocolate mixture. Scrape the sauce into a bowl or jar and cover with plastic wrap, pressing the plastic against the surface of the sauce. The sauce can be served after it has cooled for 20 minutes. (You can make this sauce up to 3 weeks in advance, cover it well, and keep it refrigerated.)

SERVING: Serve the waffles from the warming oven or from the cooling rack, in which case the chocolate chips will have had a chance to firm slightly and will provide another bit of crunch. Either way, these are sensational topped with a scoop of ice cream and some of the delicious Hot Fudge Sauce. If you've made the sauce ahead, reheat it briefly in a microwave or in the top of a double boiler set over hot, not boiling, water. Even though the 4½-inch square Belgian waffles are small, one waffle to a child, topped with ice cream and Hot Fudge Sauce, makes a good-size portion.

Tutti-Frutti Waffles

These soothingly soft, fruit-filled waffles are equally irresistible with maple syrup for breakfast or Banana-Berry Sauce for dessert. The small pieces of apple, pear, and banana that are folded into the batter are baked and softened by the iron's heat, intensifying their natural sweetness and strengthening their flavors so they taste much the way they would have had you baked them into your best pie.

PLAN AHEAD: **Prepare the sauce before you start making the waffles.**

The Waffles

4 tablespoons (½ stick)
  unsalted butter
1 cup all-purpose flour
½ cup whole-wheat flour
2 teaspoons double-acting
  baking powder
¼ cup granulated sugar
2 tablespoons firmly packed
  light brown sugar
1 cup milk
¾ cup fresh orange juice
2 large eggs
1 teaspoon pure vanilla extract
1 small apple, peeled, cored,
  and cut into small dice

1 small Bartlett, Anjou, or
  Comice pear, peeled, cored,
  and cut into small dice
1 small banana, peeled and cut
  into small dice

Maple syrup for topping if
  you're serving these at breakfast
Ice cream for accompaniment
  if you're serving these for
  dessert

MAKES ABOUT FIVE 6½-INCH ROUND WAFFLES

❶ Preheat your waffle iron. If you want to hold the finished waffles until serving time, preheat your oven to 200°F.

❷ Melt the butter; reserve. In a large bowl, whisk together the flours, baking powder, and sugars. In another bowl, whisk together the milk, orange juice, eggs, and vanilla until well combined. Pour the liquid ingredients over the dry ingredients and whisk until just mixed. Stir in the diced fruit and fold in the melted butter.

❸ Lightly butter or spray the grids of your iron, if needed. Brush or spray the grids again only if subsequent waffles stick.

❹ Spoon out a generous ½ cup of batter (or the amount recommended by your waffler's manufacturer) onto the iron. Gently spread the batter over the grids with a metal spatula or wooden spoon. Close the lid and bake until the waffle is browned and set. Serve the waffles immediately or keep them, in a single layer, on a rack in the preheated oven while you make the rest of the batch.

Topping: Banana-Berry Sauce

A sauce made by whirring sweetened berries in a blender or food processor is one of the simplest and best-tasting dessert toppings you can make. Add a banana and a squeeze of fresh lemon juice to the mix and you'll have a sweeter, creamier sauce that will blend beautifully with the fruit flavors in the waffle; it will also soften the flavor of the berries, making them thoroughly kid-friendly. If you have an ice-cream maker, you can freeze this mixture to make a wonderful sorbet to serve on top of or alongside the waffles.

One 12-ounce package frozen strawberries or raspberries in syrup, thawed (still frosty is fine)

2 bananas, peeled
Juice of ½ lemon

Place all the ingredients in the workbowl of a food processor or a blender and process until smooth, scraping down the sides as needed. Serve immediately, chill, or freeze in an ice-cream maker following the manufacturer's instructions.

SERVING: If you're serving these at breakfast, plan on one or two waffles to a child with a topping of pure maple syrup. These are also delicious accompanied by a few strips of crispy bacon. For dessert, one waffle per child is plenty. Serve with a scoop of vanilla ice cream and the Banana-Berry Sauce or, if you've frozen the sauce, replace the ice cream with a scoop of Banana-Berry Sorbet.

Honey-Yogurt Waffles

These hearty waffles are simple, straightforward, and wonderful at breakfast. The soft, lightly browned waffles get their slightly chewy texture from a mixture of grains, including whole-wheat flour and oats; their tenderness from a combination of milk and yogurt; and their sweetness from pure honey. They're delicious with maple syrup or more honey, and lovely with fresh fruit.

3 tablespoons unsalted butter
1 cup all-purpose flour
½ cup whole-wheat flour
¼ cup old-fashioned oats
   (*not* quick oats)
2 teaspoons double-acting
   baking powder
¼ teaspoon baking soda
¼ teaspoon ground cinnamon
   (optional)

1¼ cups milk
¾ cup plain yogurt
⅓ cup honey
2 large eggs
½ teaspoon pure vanilla extract

Maple syrup or honey for
   topping

MAKES ABOUT SIX 6½-INCH ROUND WAFFLES

❶ Preheat your waffle iron. If you want to hold the finished waffles until serving time, preheat your oven to 200°F.

❷ Melt the butter; reserve. In a large bowl, whisk together the flours, oats, baking powder, baking soda, and cinnamon, if you're using it. In another bowl, whisk together the milk, yogurt, honey, eggs, and vanilla until very well blended. Pour the liquid ingredients over the dry ingredients and whisk until just combined. Fold in the melted butter.

❸ Lightly butter or spray the grids of your iron, if needed. Brush or spray the grids again only if subsequent waffles stick.

❹ Spoon out a hefty ½ cup of batter (or a little more than your waffler's manufacturer recommends) onto the grids, spreading the batter evenly over the grids with a metal spatula or wooden spoon. Close the lid and bake until the waffle is golden and set. Serve the waffles immediately or keep them, in a single layer, on a rack in the preheated oven while you make the rest of the batch.

SERVING: Serve the waffles hot with a topping of maple syrup or honey. These are also good with Rosy Applesauce (page 101), jam, or fruit-flavored syrups. For a real change, think about serving these as the "bread" for a tuna salad sandwich: Leave out the cinnamon in the recipe, spread each waffle with a thin layer of mustard, fill with lettuce, tomato, and tuna salad, and serve the sandwiches with carrot and celery sticks. They're great for lunch.

Apple Waffles

If your children are fans of apple pie, they'll love these. They're made with the spices that earned apple pie its reputation—cinnamon, allspice, and freshly grated nutmeg—and they're soft, like the best foods from our childhood. Much of their appeal comes from grating a single apple into the batter and allowing the short, thin shreds of fruit to melt and spread their sweetness throughout. These are doubly good topped with a few spoonfuls of Rosy Applesauce.

PLAN AHEAD: The Rosy Applesauce can be made up to 1 week before the waffles; cover and refrigerate.

The Waffles

3 tablespoons unsalted butter
1½ cups all-purpose flour
2 teaspoons double-acting
    baking powder
1 teaspoon ground cinnamon
¼ teaspoon ground allspice
Pinch of grated nutmeg
¼ cup granulated sugar
¼ cup firmly packed light
    brown sugar

1½ cups milk
2 large eggs
1 teaspoon pure vanilla extract
1 medium-size apple, peeled
    and grated

Ice cream or lightly sweetened
    whipped cream for topping
    (optional)

MAKES ABOUT SIX 6½-INCH ROUND WAFFLES

❶ Preheat your waffle iron. If you want to hold the finished waffles until serving time, preheat your oven to 200°F.

❷ Melt the butter; reserve. In a large bowl, whisk together the flour, baking powder, spices, and sugars (make sure the brown sugar is free of lumps before adding it to the bowl). In another bowl, whisk together the milk, eggs, and vanilla until very well blended. Add the liquid ingredients to the dry ingredients and stir with the whisk until just combined. Fold in the grated apple and the melted butter.

❸ Whether or not your iron's grids are well seasoned or made of a nonstick material, it's best to lightly butter or spray the grids of your waffle iron since this batter is very soft and can stick. Brush or spray the grids again only if subsequent waffles stick.

❹ Spoon out ½ cup of batter (or the amount recommended by your waffler's manufacturer) onto the iron. Spread the batter evenly over the grids with a metal spatula or wooden spoon and close the lid. When the underside of the waffle is lightly browned, carefully turn over the waffle—these are very soft, so you may have to gently "peel" the waffle off the iron with a fork and metal spatula—and brown the other side. Serve the waffles immediately or keep them, in a single layer, on a rack in the preheated oven while you make the rest of the batch.

Topping: Rosy Applesauce

The is the best and simplest homemade applesauce I know. Because it is made with only red apples and a few drops of water, it has a fresh, fall-harvest flavor, a smooth, slide-through-your-teeth texture, and a light, rosy color that comes from simmering the apples, skin and all.

3 large red apples (McIntosh, Empire, Rome, or Cortland apples are fine)

3 tablespoons water

❶ Cut each apple into eighths and put the pieces in a heavy-bottomed 2-quart saucepan. Don't worry about pits, core, or apple peel. They'll be strained out after cooking, and during cooking they'll give the sauce extra flavor and color. Add the water and bring the mixture to a simmer over medium-low heat. Cover the pot and cook at a steady, gentle simmer until the apples fall apart when pressed with the back of a spoon, about 20 minutes. Stir with a spoon and, if the apples mash into a sauce but the mixture looks too liquidy, keep the pot uncovered on the heat for another 3 to 5 minutes, stirring as the sauce cooks.

❷ If you have a food mill fitted with a medium blade, use it to strain and smooth the applesauce. If not, press the sauce through a strainer to remove the skin, core, and pits. The sauce should be fairly smooth and not very thick. If it looks too thin, cook away the excess liquid, stirring all the while. Pour the finished sauce into a clean jar or bowl and top with a piece of plastic wrap pressed against the surface. You can serve this warm, at room temperature, or chilled.

SERVING: Serve the waffles warm, one to a child, with a generous topping of Rosy Applesauce. It wouldn't be too much to add ice cream or lightly sweetened whipped cream to this luscious dessert.

Butterscotch Babies

Butterscotch is vanilla-scented, brown-sugar sweet, caramel-colored, and the ideal flavor to blend into a dessert waffle. Eaten warm, these firm-crusted waffles have all the appeal of comfort food: Their soft interior is dotted with melted butterscotch chips; at room temperature, when the chips firm slightly, they are an irresistible cross between cookies and candy.

PLAN AHEAD: **Make the Melted Ice-Cream Sauce before you start making the waffles.**

The Waffles

3 tablespoons unsalted butter	1 cup milk
1 cup all-purpose flour	1 large egg
1 teaspoon double-acting	½ teaspoon pure vanilla extract
baking powder	½ cup butterscotch chips,
¼ teaspoon ground cinnamon	coarsely chopped
¼ cup firmly packed light	
brown sugar	

MAKES ABOUT FOUR 6½-INCH ROUND WAFFLES

❶ Preheat your waffle iron. If you want to hold the finished waffles until serving time, preheat your oven to 200°F.

❷ Melt the butter; reserve. In a large bowl, whisk together the flour, baking powder, cinnamon, and brown sugar (make certain it's free of lumps before adding it to the bowl). In another bowl, whisk together the milk, egg, and vanilla until very well blended. Stir the liquid ingredients into the dry ingredients, mixing only until combined. Fold in the chopped butterscotch chips and melted butter.

❸ Whether or not your iron's grids are well seasoned or made of a nonstick material, it is important to lightly butter or spray the grids before making the first waffle since the butterscotch chips can be sticky when they melt. You will probably have to butter or spray the grids before pouring out the batter for each waffle. (If the chips melt into the grids, don't try to do the cleanup while the iron is hot. Just butter or spray the grids and continue making the waffles.)

❹ Spoon out ½ cup of batter (or the amount recommended by your waffler's manufacturer) onto the iron. Use a metal spatula or wooden spoon to spread the batter evenly over the grids. Close the lid and bake until the underside of the waffle is lightly browned and crisp. Carefully turn the waffle over and continue baking until the other side is browned as well. Serve the waffles immediately, let them cool to room temperature, or keep them warm, in a single layer, on a rack in the preheated oven while you make the rest of the batch.

Topping: Melted Ice-Cream Sauce

This is exactly what it says it is—a sauce made by melting ice cream. It is a simple, sensible, and delicious way to dress up so many types of desserts. It works beautifully because the base of high-quality ice cream is a crème anglaise, or custard sauce, the same kind of sauce pastry chefs use to enhance their most elaborate creations. By doing nothing more than placing a container of ice cream on the counter, you can have a luscious sauce that's as right for this child-pleasing waffle as it is for your most sophisticated sweets.

    1 pint premium-quality vanilla
    ice cream

You want to serve this sauce cold and almost completely melted. To melt the ice cream, leave the container in a bowl on the kitchen counter for about 30 minutes, or until it is almost melted and still cool.

SERVING: These waffles can be served straight off the iron (actually, you should wait a couple of minutes before serving them to children since the chips get very hot), warm, or at room temperature. Whichever way you choose, give each kid a generous amount of Melted Ice-Cream Sauce. I think vanilla is the best flavor to serve with butterscotch because it fortifies the brown sugar and vanilla flavors that make butterscotch so appealing, but if there's a flavor you prefer, you can use that flavor for the sauce or, if you really want to spoil your kids, pour the vanilla Melted Ice-Cream Sauce on the plate, put the waffle on the sauce in the center of the plate, and then top with a scoop of a different flavor ice cream.

Waffle Pizzas

These individual pizzas make great lunches and very special afternoon snacks. The topping is classic: tomato sauce, mozzarella cheese, and a dusting of Parmesan. The "crust," however, is innovative—a waffle robustly accented with oregano, thyme, and freshly grated Parmesan cheese. Thanks to the addition of pasta flour, the waffle's crust and inner sponge are quite sturdy. While these will never replace brick-oven pizzas, they will become family favorites, especially if you personalize the toppings.

The Waffles

1 cup all-purpose flour
⅓ cup pasta flour (semolina flour)
1½ teaspoons double-acting baking powder
1 teaspoon salt
1 teaspoon dried oregano leaves or 1 tablespoon fresh
½ teaspoon dried thyme or 2 teaspoons fresh

½ teaspoon freshly ground black pepper
3 tablespoons freshly grated Parmesan cheese
1¼ cups milk
2 large eggs
3 tablespoons extra-virgin olive oil

MAKES ABOUT FIVE 6½-INCH ROUND WAFFLES

❶ Preheat your waffle iron. When you are ready to serve the pizza waffles, you'll need to preheat the oven to 375°F.

❷ In a large bowl, whisk together the flours, baking powder, salt, oregano, thyme, pepper, and Parmesan to mix. In another bowl, whisk together the milk and eggs until well blended. Pour the liquid ingredients over the dry ingredients and stir with the whisk until just combined. Fold in the olive oil.

❸ Lightly butter or spray the grids of your iron, if needed. Brush or spray the grids again only if subsequent waffles stick.

❹ Spoon out ½ cup of batter (or the amount recommended by your waffler's manufacturer) onto the iron. Use a metal spatula or wooden spoon to spread the batter evenly over the grids. Close the lid and bake until the waffle is firm, crisp, and pale golden. Keep on a cooling rack while you make the rest of the batch. (You can make these waffles early in the day, wrap them well, and refrigerate them, or you can wrap them airtight and freeze them for up to 1 month.)

Topping: Pizza Topping

This is the topping for the kind of pizza most of us grew up with—tomato sauce and melted cheese. If you want to turn these into the now-popular "designer" pizzas or personalize them so they include your family's most favored ingredients, you can do so easily. Think about putting peppers, slices of pepperoni, or pieces of lightly steamed vegetables over the tomato sauce and strewing the topping with different kinds of cheese (small dollops of fresh ricotta or shreds of cheddar are good choices).

1⅔ cups meatless tomato sauce (homemade or store-bought)
1½ cups shredded mozzarella cheese
⅓ cup freshly grated Parmesan cheese

1½ tablespoons olive oil
Salt and freshly ground black pepper to taste

Preheat your oven to 375°F. Place the waffles on a foil-lined baking sheet. Divide the sauce among the waffles, using a metal spatula to spread the sauce evenly over each waffle. Sprinkle each waffle with equal amounts of mozzarella and Parmesan cheese and drizzle over a little olive oil. Season with salt and pepper and bake until the waffles are heated through and the cheese is melted and bubbly, about 8 to 12 minutes. (You will need to bake the pizzas longer if the waffles have been chilled or frozen; if the cheese starts to brown before the waffles are hot, cover the waffles loosely with a sheet of aluminum foil.) Serve immediately.

SERVING: These are hearty, so I suggest you serve each child one Waffle Pizza and a portion of green salad. If you have a larger group to serve, just double or triple the recipes.

Ham-and-Cheese Waffle Sandwiches

The cheddar cheese waffles that provide the "bread" for these sandwiches are golden brown and dairy rich with a flavor reminiscent of a cheese omelet. They bake crisp and soften appealingly as they cool, attaining just the right texture to be spread with mustard and filled with honey-baked ham, slices of cheddar, and crisp lettuce. This recipe makes two very generous sandwiches; double or triple the recipe if you need more.

The Waffles

3 tablespoons unsalted butter	1¼ cups milk
1 cup all-purpose flour	2 large eggs
1½ teaspoons double-acting	⅔ cup (about 3 ounces)
baking powder	shredded cheddar cheese
¼ teaspoon salt	(you can use white or yellow
Pinch of cayenne pepper	cheddar, but the yellow gives
Freshly ground black pepper to	the waffles a sunnier color)
taste	

MAKES ABOUT FOUR 6½-INCH ROUND WAFFLES

❶ Preheat your waffle iron.

❷ Melt the butter; reserve. In a large bowl, whisk together the flour, baking powder, salt, and peppers to mix. In another bowl, whisk together the milk and eggs until well blended. Pour the liquid ingredients over the dry ingredients and stir with the whisk until just combined. Fold in the shredded cheese and melted butter.

❸ Lightly butter or spray the grids of your iron, if needed. Brush or spray the grids again only if subsequent waffles stick.

❹ Spoon out ½ cup of batter (or the amount recommended by your waffler's manufacturer) onto the grids, spreading it evenly with a metal spatula or wooden spoon. Close the lid and bake until the waffle is golden and set. Keep the waffles, in a single layer, on a cooling rack while you make the rest of the batch. You can make sandwiches with these waffles when they are hot, warm, or at room temperature. If you've made them early in the day and want to warm them before using, put them on a baking sheet, in a single layer, cover loosely with aluminum foil, and heat for about 5 minutes in a 350°F oven.

Filling: Ham and Cheese

Honey-baked ham, some slices of cheddar, crunchy lettuce, ripe tomato, and sharp mustard make a terrific filling for these sandwiches. But there's no reason to limit yourself. The waffles blend with salty meats like salami, bologna, and bacon (think about a BLT on these waffles), as well as with assorted vegetables, such as roasted peppers, crisp cucumbers, zucchini, and sprouts. Try this savory ham-and-cheese filling first, then be creative and find the combinations your children love most.

Mustard (Dijon or American-style)
Romaine lettuce
6 slices honey-baked ham or other full-flavored sliced ham

4 slices cheddar cheese
1 ripe tomato, thinly sliced

Spread one side of each waffle with mustard. Divide the remaining ingredients evenly between 2 waffles. Cover, mustard side down, with the 2 other waffles and cut each sandwich into quarters.

SERVING: Served alongside a bowl of vegetable soup, these sandwiches make a delicious fall or winter lunch. Since the sandwiches are substantial, you might want to count on half portions, especially if you're serving the children soup, too.

4

Snacks and Starters

Waffle Chips, Hors d'Oeuvres, and Appetizers

Like just about everyone I know, I am busier than ever and entertain a lot less grandly than I used to. These days, I invite friends for drinks and nibbles, a casual buffet, or a simple supper far more frequently than I arrange many-course dinner parties. With this kind of entertaining, I look for fun, tasty foods that are quick to make, and waffles fit this bill. ❡ I'd never thought of waffles as party food until I started working on this book—and then I couldn't stop. If the Italians could use toasted bread for crostini and bruschetta, I wondered why waffles couldn't serve the same purpose. And if corn, potato, and vegetable chips were being dipped into everything from salsas to purees, why couldn't the same be done with crispy waffles? ❡ The snack waffles I created here and call waffle chips are waffles that are baked again in a slow oven. Their crunchy, flavorful bite does everything crackers, chips, and toasts do—but better. ❡ You can fill a basket with Cilantro Waffle Chips to serve with guacamole when friends come over to root for the home team on TV. Or, you can pass plates of Tuscan White Bean Waffle Chips, redolent of garlic, before a backyard barbecue. And when you do have the time for a dress-up cock-tail party, you can dress up these waffle recipes. Basil-Parmesan Waffle Chips with Balsamic Tomatoes is glamorous enough for your best china. ¶ These waffle recipes can be doubled, tripled, and even quadrupled, so they're great for a crowd. You can make the chips ahead because they keep at room temperature for 3 days. Soft waffles, like the exotically spiced Couscous Waffles, can al-ways be kept in the freezer, ready for the next party. Knowing that party food can be so easy to make is bound to encourage you to have your next party soon.

Cilantro Waffle Chips
with Chunky Guacamole

No matter how many Cilantro Waffle Chips you make, and how much guacamole you put out, you'll wish you'd made more. These waffles go as fast as the nacho chips they were created to replace. They start out as scrumptious, highly seasoned cornmeal waffles spiked with pieces of fresh jalapeño, then they're baked slowly in the oven until they become crisp like a cracker. The results are revolutionary—a spicy, peppery chip that gets its snap and crunch without frying. I make these in a five-of-hearts waffle iron, the better to get them thin and crusty, but you can make them in any kind of waffler. All you've got to do is cut them into snack-size squares before putting them in the oven. The recipes for both the waffles and guacamole can be multiplied, so think of these when you're expecting a crowd.

PLAN AHEAD: You can make the guacamole before or after the chips are baked.

The Waffles

1 tablespoon unsalted butter
½ cup all-purpose flour
½ cup cornmeal
1¼ teaspoons double-acting
   baking powder
¼ teaspoon baking soda
¼ teaspoon salt
⅛ teaspoon freshly ground
   black pepper

1 cup buttermilk
1 large egg
¼ cup chopped fresh cilantro
1 teaspoon finely chopped
   jalapeño pepper
2 tablespoons corn oil

Sour cream or plain yogurt for
   additional topping

MAKES ABOUT 4 FULL FIVE-OF-HEARTS WAFFLES

❶ Preheat your waffle iron. Preheat your oven to 200°F.

❷ Melt the butter; reserve. In a large bowl, whisk together the flour, cornmeal, baking powder, baking soda, salt, and pepper to mix. In another bowl, beat together the buttermilk and egg until well blended and whisk into the dry ingredients. Stir in the cilantro and jalapeño. Fold in the corn oil and melted butter, mixing only until combined.

continued

❸ Lightly butter or spray the grids of your waffle iron, if needed. Brush or spray the grids again only if subsequent waffles stick.

❹ Spoon out ½ cup of batter (or the amount your waffler's manufacturer suggests) onto the iron, spreading it evenly to the edge of the grids with a metal spatula or wooden spoon. Close the lid and bake until golden and crispy. Remove the waffle from the iron and separate into hearts or cut into whatever size pieces you want. Place on a baking sheet, in a single layer, and put into the preheated oven. Continue making the rest of the batch and putting the finished waffles on the sheet in the oven. The waffles should bake in the oven for 1 to 1½ hours, or until they are very crispy. Serve immediately or cool on a rack and serve at room temperature. (The waffles can be made up to 3 days ahead and stored at room temperature in a loosely covered tin.)

Topping: Chunky Guacamole

Saucy and sassy, this Chunky Guacamole is a bright, fresh mix of diced vegetables, hot pepper, and creamy avocado, tossed rather than mashed, so that each ingredient retains its crunch and characteristic bite. While I prefer the flavor of Hass avocados (the small avocados whose pebbly skins turn almost black when they're ripe), you can make a delicious guacamole with any variety as long as the avocado is ripe and you add it to the mixture at the last minute—"cooking" in lime juice for too long will spoil the taste and texture of an avocado, no matter how perfect it is at the start.

3 plum tomatoes or 1 large tomato, seeded and finely diced	½ teaspoon peeled, finely chopped garlic
2 scallions, white part only, trimmed and thinly sliced	Juice of ½ lime (or more to taste)
½ red bell pepper, seeded, deveined, and finely diced	Salt and freshly ground black pepper to taste
½ jalapeño pepper, seeded, deveined, and finely chopped	1 tablespoon finely chopped fresh cilantro
	1 ripe avocado

Place all the ingredients *except* the avocado in a nonreactive bowl and stir to mix. Cover and set aside until serving time. (You can make this up to 2 hours ahead. Cover it well and refrigerate until needed.) Right before serving, peel, pit, and cut the avocado into small cubes; gently stir into the guacamole.

SERVING: Arrange the waffles on a large platter or pile them into a basket as you would chips. Spoon the guacamole into one bowl and the sour cream into another and encourage guests to put a dollop of each on a waffle chip and dig in. These are great with a bucket of grilled shrimp or shrimp boiled in their shells. Pass around a pitcher of ice-cold beer and you've got a party.

Summer Corn and Sweet Pepper Waffles
with Corn Confetti Salsa

Corn kernels fresh from the cob, sweet, juicy, and smelling of sunshine and soil, are one of summer's great joys, and here they are served two ways: baked into tangy cornmeal-buttermilk waffles and mixed into a colorful, chile-sparked salsa. The corn kernels speckling the waffles' interior retain their slight crunch and full summery sweetness, while the light-crusted waffles are pliable, like a soft tortilla. You can also crisp these in a slow oven.

PLAN AHEAD: Make the salsa as close to serving time as possible.

The Waffles

2 ears yellow or white corn, husked

1 red bell pepper, seeded, deveined, and finely diced

½ jalapeño pepper (or more to taste), seeded, deveined, and finely chopped

4 tablespoons (½ stick) unsalted butter

1 cup all-purpose flour

½ cup yellow cornmeal

2 teaspoons double-acting baking powder

½ teaspoon baking soda

½ teaspoon salt

¼ teaspoon freshly ground black pepper

Pinch of cayenne pepper (optional)

Pinch of chili powder (optional)

1½ cups buttermilk

2 large eggs

MAKES ABOUT 6 FULL FIVE-OF-HEARTS WAFFLES

❶ Preheat your waffle iron. If you want to hold the finished waffles until serving time or to crisp them, preheat your oven to 200°F.

❷ Working over a bowl and using a small sharp knife, slash each row of corn kernels down the middle from top to bottom, then cut the kernels from the cob, working close to the fibrous cob but not cutting into it. Add the diced red pepper and jalapeño to the bowl; set aside.

❸ Melt the butter; reserve. In a large bowl, whisk together the flour, cornmeal, baking powder, baking soda, salt, pepper, and optional seasonings. In another bowl, beat together the buttermilk and eggs with a whisk until well blended. Pour the liquid ingredients over the dry ingredients and whisk just to combine. Stir in the reserved corn mixture and then the melted butter.

❹ Lightly butter or spray the grids of your waffle iron, if needed. Brush or spray the grids again only if subsequent waffles stick.

❺ Spoon out a full ½ cup of batter (or the amount recommended by your waffler's manufacturer) onto the grids. This batter is thickish and needs to be nudged to the edge of the grid with a metal spatula or wooden spoon. Close the lid and bake until lightly golden and crisped. Remove the waffle and cut into dip-size pieces. Then transfer them to a cooling rack so they can be served at room temperature, keep them warm in the preheated oven while you make the rest of the waffles, or bake them in the preheated oven for about 30 minutes to crisp before serving. (If you decide to crisp these, don't overbake them—remember, they won't become super-crunchy—and do serve them shortly after removing them from the oven. If you wait too long, the corn kernels can become tough.)

Topping: Corn-Confetti Salsa

Sweet yellow corn, crunchy peppers of many colors, puckery lime juice, and fresh herbs brighten this irresistible salsa. If you can, try to make the salsa as close to serving time as possible so the corn will retain its crunch, color, and flavor.

1 cup fresh corn kernels from 1 to 2 ears of corn (see page 116 for directions for removing kernels from cob)
½ red bell pepper, seeded, deveined, and finely diced
½ green bell pepper, seeded, deveined, and finely diced
½ yellow bell pepper, seeded, deveined, and finely diced
½ jalapeño pepper, seeded, deveined, and finely diced

3 scallions, white part only, finely sliced, or ½ small red onion, peeled and finely diced
Juice from 1 lime
½ teaspoon salt
Pinch of chili powder
Dash of cayenne pepper
2 teaspoons corn or olive oil
2 teaspoons finely minced fresh cilantro
2 teaspoons finely minced fresh parsley

continued

Put all the ingredients in a nonreactive medium-size bowl and toss to mix. Serve immediately or refrigerate, covered, up to 2 hours.

SERVING: Serve these just the way you'd serve crackers and a saucy topping, turning the waffles into a basket or arranging them on a plate and presenting the salsa in a bowl with a spoon. These are fine as a stand-up hors d'oeuvre at a cocktail party since they need just napkins stacked near the salsa, and they're great before a barbecue.

Couscous Waffles with Roasted Pepper Dip

The main ingredient in these extraordinary waffles is quick-cooking semolina couscous, a staple throughout Morocco. The couscous is seasoned with cinnamon, ginger, cumin, and turmeric (which is responsible for its gorgeous color) and cooked in chicken broth so that it softens and absorbs the spices. Mixed into the waffle batter and baked, it produces an interior sponge that is soft and slightly grainy. If you want to serve these as an hors d'oeuvre or snack, it is best to make heart-shaped waffles or to cut waffles of other shapes into smaller sizes. But if you want to serve these as a sit-down starter before a dinner party, try to make them in a Belgian waffler so you can get the full measure of couscous' sensual texture in the waffles' thick centers and deep pockets.

PLAN AHEAD: The Roasted Pepper Dip should be made before the waffles.

The Waffles

1 cup chicken broth	1 cup chicken broth
1 tablespoon extra-virgin olive oil	1 large egg
1 teaspoon ground cinnamon	1 cup all-purpose flour
½ teaspoon ground ginger	2 teaspoons double-acting baking powder
½ teaspoon ground cumin	½ teaspoon salt
¼ teaspoon ground turmeric	2 tablespoons extra-virgin olive oil
½ cup quick-cooking or instant couscous	

MAKES ABOUT 5 FULL FIVE-OF-HEARTS WAFFLES

❶ Bring the 1 cup chicken broth, 1 tablespoon olive oil, and the spices to the boil in a medium-size saucepan over medium heat. Slowly and gradually add the couscous, stirring all the while. Reduce the heat to low and cook, stirring, for 1 minute. Remove the saucepan from the heat, cover, and set aside until the couscous has absorbed all the liquid, about 5 minutes.

❷ Preheat your waffle iron. If you want to hold the finished waffles until serving time, preheat your oven to 200°F.

continued

❸ Turn the couscous into a large bowl and stir with a fork to separate the grains. (If there are large clumps, break them up with your fingers.) Whisk in the remaining 1 cup chicken broth and the egg, beating until well blended. In a small bowl, whisk together the flour, baking powder, and salt to combine. Pour this over the couscous and stir until just incorporated. Fold in the 2 tablespoons olive oil.

❹ Lightly butter or spray the grids of your waffle iron, if needed. Brush or spray the grids again only if subsequent waffles stick.

❺ Spoon out ½ cup of batter (or the amount recommended by your waffler's manufacturer) onto the grids. Spread the batter evenly across the grids with a metal spatula or wooden spoon. Close the lid and bake until the waffle is golden and the crust is quite firm. Serve the waffles immediately or keep them, in a single layer, on a rack in the preheated oven while you make the rest of the batch.

Topping: Roasted Pepper Dip

The dominant flavor in this lusty sauce is roasted sweet red peppers, with hot chile pepper, garlic, and briny black olives added for extra vibrancy. The sauce is easily made in a blender or food processor and smoothed with cottage cheese, which binds and mellows the mixture. If you adore roasted red peppers, omit the cottage cheese and double all the other ingredients.

One 7-ounce jar roasted red peppers, drained and patted dry, or an equivalent amount of freshly roasted and skinned peppers
1 large plump garlic clove, peeled and pressed
½ hot red chile pepper, seeded, deveined, and minced

1 tablespoon extra-virgin olive oil
1 teaspoon tomato paste
Salt and freshly ground black pepper to taste
Pinch of sugar
½ pound cottage cheese
12 black olives, pitted (optional)

Place all the ingredients *except* the cottage cheese and olives in the workbowl of a food processor or blender. Process until smooth, scraping down the sides of the container as necessary. Add the cottage cheese and continue to process until well blended and creamy. Add the olives, if you're using them, and pulse several times to chop and distribute evenly. The dip is ready to serve. (It can be made up to 5 days in advance, covered, and kept refrigerated.)

SERVING: Although the waffles are tasty at room temperature, they're at their peak piping hot. Spoon the dip into a small serving bowl, place on a platter, and arrange the hot waffles around the dip, inviting everyone to take a waffle, scoop up some dip, and enjoy the pair out of hand. The combination of Couscous Waffles and dip is so complex that you can choose several different beverages as accompaniment; white wine, minty iced tea, or well-chilled beer each makes a good match to this dish.

Super-Crunchy Masa Harina Waffle Chips
with Mango-Ginger Salsa

It's the masa harina that gives these waffles their crunch as well as their absolutely singular flavor. Distinctly not-sweet masa harina, which is finely milled corn flour, is the primary ingredient in tortillas, and those familiar with the Mexican pancake will taste in these waffles a strong corn flavor that is immediately recognizable as the taste that makes tortillas so widely beloved. You can bake these a bit longer in the waffle iron and serve them warm, but they're really best well baked in the iron and then rebaked in an oven so that their golden crust is crisper, their inner sponge firmer, and their corn flavor more pronounced.
They are the perfect partner for the bracing Mango-Ginger Salsa.
When you want these for a party, just multiply the recipes.

PLAN AHEAD: The waffle chips should be made and crisped in the oven before the salsa is prepared.

The Waffles

½ cup masa harina	⅛ teaspoon freshly ground
½ cup all-purpose flour	black pepper
1¼ teaspoons double-acting	Pinch of cayenne pepper
baking powder	1 cup milk
½ teaspoon salt	1 large egg
	2 tablespoons corn oil

MAKES ABOUT 4 FULL FIVE-OF-HEARTS WAFFLES

❶ Preheat your waffle iron. If you want to hold the finished waffles until serving time or to crisp them, preheat your oven to 200°F.

❷ In a large bowl, whisk together the masa harina, flour, baking powder, salt, pepper, and cayenne to combine. In another bowl, whisk together the milk and egg to blend very well. Pour the liquid ingredients over the dry ingredients and whisk until just mixed. Fold in the corn oil.

❸ Lightly butter or spray the grids of your waffle iron, if needed. Brush or spray the grids again only if subsequent waffles stick.

❹ Spoon out ½ cup of batter (or the amount recommended by your waffler's manufacturer) onto the grids, spreading the batter evenly across the iron with a metal spatula or wooden spoon. Close the lid and bake until the waffle is deeply golden and crisped. Cut the waffle into hearts or snack-size pieces and place, in a single layer, directly on a rack in the preheated oven; continue making the remaining waffles. Bake the waffles for 1 hour, or until they are firm and resemble crackers. Transfer to a cooling rack and cool to room temperature. (The waffles can be made up to 3 days ahead and stored at room temperature in a loosely covered tin.)

Topping: Mango-Ginger Salsa

Mango-Ginger Salsa is a spirited combination of golden-fleshed mango, sweet-spicy fresh ginger, refreshing lime juice, and the jewels of Mexican seasoning—jalapeño pepper and cilantro. Make sure you choose ripe juicy mangoes and treat them with the care they deserve: Keep the mangoes at room temperature; wash the skins before cutting them; and cut away the fruit from the pits, making sure to separate the flesh from the "strings." Give the salsa ½ hour to macerate and meld flavors, but don't let it wait too long before serving or the mangoes will lose their luster and lushness.

2 ripe mangoes, pitted, peeled, and cut into small dice
2 tablespoons finely chopped red onion
2 teaspoons peeled, finely chopped fresh ginger
1 jalapeño pepper, seeded, deveined, and minced
Juice of 1 lime (or more or less to taste)
1 tablespoon finely chopped fresh cilantro

Put all the ingredients *except* the cilantro into a nonreactive medium bowl and stir with a rubber spatula to combine. Allow the salsa to macerate for no more than 30 minutes. Stir in the cilantro just before serving.

SERVING: These are a showstopper at cocktail parties, great with margaritas or iced tea. Just pile the chips into a napkin-lined basket, put the salsa close by so guests can spoon some over their chips, and have some colorful small napkins on hand.

Basil-Parmesan Waffle Chips
with Balsamic Tomatoes

Bruschetta, garlic toast brushed with olive oil and topped with chopped tomatoes, was the inspiration for this combination. The outstanding flavors in the chips are Parmesan, extra-virgin olive oil, and fresh basil. Like bruschetta, these are wonderful with drinks or ideal as the first course for a casual dinner.

PLAN AHEAD: Make the waffle chips and crisp them in the oven before you make the topping.

The Waffles

⅔ cup all-purpose flour
⅓ cup pasta flour (semolina flour)
1¼ teaspoons double-acting baking powder
¾ teaspoon salt
1¼ cups milk
1 large egg

½ cup packed fresh basil leaves, chopped or shredded
¼ cup freshly grated Parmesan cheese
3 tablespoons extra-virgin olive oil

Fresh basil leaves for garnish

MAKES ABOUT 5 FULL FIVE-OF-HEARTS WAFFLES

❶ Preheat your waffle iron. If you want to crisp the waffles, preheat your oven to 200°F.

❷ In a large bowl, whisk together the flours, baking powder, and salt to combine. In another bowl, whisk together the milk and egg until very well blended. Pour the liquid ingredients over the dry ingredients and stir with the whisk until just mixed. Fold in the basil, Parmesan, and olive oil.

❸ Lightly butter or spray the grids of your waffle iron, if needed. Brush or spray the grids again only if subsequent waffles stick.

❹ Spoon out ½ cup of batter (or the amount recommended by your waffler's manufacturer) onto the grids. Spread the batter evenly across the iron with a metal spatula or wooden spoon. Close the lid and bake until the waffle is lightly golden and set (these will remain fairly pale). Cut into serving-size pieces, and place, in a single layer, on a rack in the preheated oven. Make the rest of the waffles. To crisp the waffles, bake them for 1 hour. (These do not become as crunchy as masa harina or cilantro waffle chips, but they will firm and dry appealingly after an hour in the oven.) Transfer the chips to a cooling rack and serve when they reach room temperature. (The waffle chips can be made up to 3 days in advance and stored at room temperature in a loosely covered tin.)

Topping: Balsamic Tomatoes

Tomatoes and balsamic vinegar have been a treasured combination for centuries. Here, the pair is mixed with basil and olive oil to produce a saucy salad that's perfect spooned over waffle chips.

4 large ripe tomatoes, juiced, seeded, and cut into small dice
1 to 2 plump garlic cloves (or to taste), peeled and finely chopped

2 tablespoons balsamic vinegar
1 tablespoon extra-virgin olive oil

Place all the ingredients in a nonreactive medium-size bowl. Stir to mix and serve within 20 minutes. (The salad will be fine if it waits longer, but it is at its best served before the tomatoes absorb too much dressing.)

SERVING: While these are great served as part of a cocktail party spread or an antipasto platter, they are fabulous before a dinner of grilled fish or sautéed seafood, pan-roasted veal or chicken cutlets. You can serve the chips family-style, with the topping passed in an attractive bowl with a spoon, or you can arrange four or five chips on individual plates, topping each chip with some tomato salad and garnishing the plates with whole basil leaves.

Blue Corn Chips with Black Bean Salsa

Blue corn is not a novelty ingredient; it is, in fact, the original type of corn raised by Native Americans. The cornmeal is, indeed, blueish, but turns a deep brown when baked in the waffle iron. Its taste suggests tartness and is slightly more reminiscent of buckwheat than cornmeal as we know it. Combined with traditional chili spices and topped with a glistening, cilantro-sparked salsa, these waffle chips make sensational party food. And, when you're planning a party, keep in mind that you can easily multiply the recipes for both the chips and salsa.

PLAN AHEAD: Because the salsa can be made a few hours ahead, you can prepare the chips and salsa in whatever order is most convenient for you.

The Waffles

½ cup blue cornmeal
½ cup all-purpose flour
1 teaspoon double-acting
  baking powder
¼ teaspoon baking soda
¼ teaspoon salt
¾ teaspoon chili powder

¼ teaspoon dried oregano
Pinch of ground cumin (more
  or less to taste)
1 cup buttermilk
1 large egg
3 tablespoons corn oil

MAKES ABOUT 4 FULL FIVE-OF-HEARTS WAFFLES

❶ Preheat your waffle iron. If you want to hold the finished waffles until serving time, preheat your oven to 200°F.

❷ In a large bowl, whisk together the cornmeal, flour, baking powder, baking soda, salt, and seasonings until mixed. In another bowl, whisk together the buttermilk and egg until well blended. Pour the liquid ingredients over the dry ingredients and stir with the whisk until just combined. Fold in the corn oil.

❸ Lightly butter or spray the grids of your waffle iron, if needed. Brush or spray the grids again only if subsequent waffles stick.

❹ Spoon out ½ cup of batter (or the amount recommended by your waffler's manufacturer) onto the grids, spreading the batter evenly across the iron with a metal spatula or wooden spoon. Close the lid and bake until the waffle is well browned and very crisp, giving the waffle a little more time than you might other waffles just to make certain it's really firm. (These can be crisped in a 200°F oven for 1 hour, but there's really no need. Just bake them well in the iron and they'll be delicious.) Transfer the crispy waffles, in a single layer, to a cooling rack and make the rest of the batch.

Topping: Black Bean Salsa

This is a multicolored mix of firm, shiny black beans, small pieces of sweet red pepper, cubes of red onion, and flecks of green jalapeño and cilantro. If the zesty flavors don't transport you to Santa Fe, the palette of colors will.

One 16-ounce can black beans, rinsed and well drained

1 small red onion, peeled and finely diced

1 red bell pepper, seeded, deveined, and finely diced

1 small hot chili pepper, such as jalapeño or serrano, seeded, deveined, and finely diced

Juice of 1 to 2 limes (more or less to taste)

Salt to taste

2 tablespoons finely chopped fresh cilantro

Mix together all the ingredients *except* the cilantro in a nonreactive medium-size mixing bowl. You can make this salsa a few hours before serving time; just stir in the cilantro at the last minute.

SERVING: Mound the Blue Corn Chips in one pottery bowl, the salsa in another, and serve with plenty of icy Mexican beer and wedges of fresh lime.

Dill Waffle Chips with Yogurt Spoon Dip

Feathery dill, its aroma as fresh as just-mowed grass, is folded into this waffle chip batter along with tangy yogurt and slices of scallions. Served hot off the grids, the waffles have a thin, inner sponge that is soft, creamy, and comforting, the way so many foods with warm onions are; baked in the oven then cooled, the chips crisp and brown like toast. Warm and soft or cool and crackery, the chips are great served with a mix of dill-scented yogurt and chopped vegetables.

PLAN AHEAD: If you're going to serve the waffle chips warm, make the spoon dip ahead. If you're going to crisp the waffles in the oven, you can make the topping at any time.

The Waffles

1 cup all-purpose flour
1¼ teaspoons double-acting
  baking powder
¼ teaspoon baking soda
½ teaspoon salt
⅔ cup plain low-fat yogurt
½ cup milk

1 large egg
3 scallions, white part only,
  trimmed and sliced very thin
3 tablespoons snipped fresh dill
2 tablespoons extra-virgin
  olive oil

MAKES ABOUT 5 FULL FIVE-OF-HEARTS WAFFLES

❶ Preheat your waffle iron. If you want to hold the finished waffles until serving time or to crisp them, preheat your oven to 200°F.

❷ In a large bowl, whisk together the flour, baking powder, baking soda, and salt just to mix. In another bowl, whisk together the yogurt, milk, and egg to blend very well. Pour the liquid ingredients over the dry ingredients and stir with the whisk to combine. Gently fold in the scallions, dill, and olive oil.

❸ Lightly butter or spray the grids of your waffle iron, if needed. Brush or spray the grids again only if subsequent waffles stick.

❹ Spoon out ½ cup of batter (or the amount recommended by your waffler's manufacturer) onto the hot iron. Use a metal spatula or wooden spoon to spread the batter evenly over the grids. Close the lid and bake until the waffle is well browned and firm. Cut it into individual hearts (if you're using a five-of-hearts waffler) or serving-size pieces, and serve immediately, keep warm, in a single layer on a rack in the preheated oven, or crisp in the oven for about 30 minutes. Continue with the rest of the batch. (If you crisp the waffles, they can be made up to 3 days ahead and kept in a loosely covered tin at room temperature.)

Topping: Yogurt Spoon Dip

This full-of-flavor combination is a cross between a dip and a creamy sauce that has to be spooned onto a cracker, hence its name. The base is tart yogurt; the additions are tiny pieces of cucumber, celery, and scallions seasoned with dill, parsley, and coarse salt. Made in minutes, the spoon dip can be kept overnight, a help if you're serving these chips and dip for brunch.

1 English (seedless) cucumber or 1 regular cucumber	1 tablespoon snipped fresh dill
1 celery rib, washed and trimmed	1 tablespoon finely chopped fresh parsley
2 scallions, white part and 1 inch of green, trimmed	½ teaspoon coarse salt
	1 cup plain low-fat yogurt

❶ Cut the cucumber in half lengthwise and remove the seeds, if necessary. Cut each half into long, very thin strips; cut the strips crosswise into a tiny dice. Use the same method to cut the celery and scallions into a tiny dice.

❷ Stir all the ingredients together in a medium-size serving bowl. Serve immediately or cover and refrigerate until needed. (This dip can be made up to 1 day ahead, covered, and refrigerated.)

SERVING: These are splendid served as part of a brunch, cocktail, or supper buffet because the combination of chips and dip can replace salad and bread. Serve the topping in a decorative bowl with a spoon. If you want to present these as part of a sit-down meal, arrange the chips around the bowl of topping on a large serving platter and pass the platter, allowing everyone to serve himself.

Tuscan White Bean Waffle Chips
with Garlicky Bean Puree

Tuscan white bean puree is a simple wonder—a smooth puree of white beans cooked in broth, seasoned with herbs, blended with aromatic olive oil, and enlivened by more than a polite amount of garlic. It's uncommonly good as the backbone of a thin, light waffle. When these waffles come off the iron, they are pale and delicately crusted, perfect topped with puree and served on a plate with knives and forks at the table. Made in a five-of-hearts waffler or cut into snack-size portions, then crisped in the oven until they resemble crackers, these waffle chips become finger food, a fabulous addition to any cocktail party buffet.

PLAN AHEAD: Make the Garlicky Bean Puree first since you will need a cup of this puree to make the waffles.

The Waffles

1 cup all-purpose flour
2 teaspoons double-acting
   baking powder
Salt and freshly ground black
   pepper to taste
1 cup Garlicky Bean Puree
   (page 131)

1¼ cups chicken broth
1 large egg
¼ cup extra-virgin olive oil

Fresh thyme, parsley sprigs, or
   small cubes of tomato for
   garnish (optional)

MAKES ABOUT 6 FULL FIVE-OF-HEARTS WAFFLES

❶ Preheat your waffle iron. If you want to hold the finished waffles until serving time or to crisp them, preheat your oven to 200°F.

❷ In a large bowl, whisk together the flour, baking powder, salt, and pepper to combine. Stir in the bean puree. In another bowl, whisk together the chicken broth, egg, and olive oil until very well mixed. Pour the liquid ingredients into the bowl with the puree mixture and stir with the whisk until just blended. The mixture will be liquidy.

❸ Lightly butter or spray the grids of your waffle iron, if needed. Brush or spray the grids again only if subsequent waffles stick.

❹ Spoon out ½ cup of batter (or the amount recommended by your waffler's manufacturer) onto the hot grids. Spread the batter evenly over the grids with a metal spatula or wooden spoon. Close the lid and bake until very lightly browned (this waffle stays pale) and set. If you plan to serve the waffles warm and uncrisped, serve them immediately or put them, in a single layer, on a rack in the preheated oven while you make the rest of the batch. If you want to serve the waffles as chips, separate them into hearts or cut them into whatever shape you want, and bake them in the preheated oven for 1 to 1½ hours. Serve when cool.

Topping: Garlicky Bean Puree

You get layer upon layer of flavor in this easily made puree. The beans for this voluptuous topping are mild, creamy white kidney beans, called cannellini, cooked in well-seasoned broth until they've absorbed all the herbs and garlic, and then pureed with extra-virgin olive oil. You can used canned beans with excellent results in this recipe, which makes enough puree to mix into the waffle chip batter and use as a dip.

Two 19-ounce cans cannellini
1 cup chicken broth
4 large plump garlic cloves, peeled and smashed with a knife
½ small yellow onion, peeled and coarsely chopped

½ teaspoon salt
¼ teaspoon dried thyme
1 small bay leaf
2 tablespoons extra-virgin olive oil

Rinse and drain the cannellini. Put all the ingredients *except* the olive oil in a 2-quart saucepan and cook over medium-low heat for 20 minutes, stirring often, until the beans are very soft and can be mashed with the back of a spoon. Remove from the heat and pour into the workbowl of a food processor or a blender. Add the olive oil and process until satiny, scraping down the sides as needed. Turn into a small bowl, press a piece of plastic wrap against the surface, and allow to come to room temperature. (The puree can be made up to 4 days in advance, covered well, and kept refrigerated.)

continued

SERVING: If you're going to serve these waffles light-crusted, soft-centered, and hot off the grids, cut each waffle into two or three pieces, depending on size (I like to cut square Belgian waffles into triangles for these), and top each with a generous layer of puree and a garnish of herbs and tomato cubes. Served this way, the waffles and puree are a polished appetizer that will set the stage for a refined dinner. Offered as chips, the waffles should be arranged on serving dishes or in baskets and the puree spooned into an attractive bowl. A hearty red wine is wonderful with these waffles.

5

Dressed for Dinner

Main-Dish Waffles and Sidekicks

Waffles for dinner may sound like a new idea to most of us—my mother served them only at breakfast—but it is actually a centuries-old tradition in America, particularly in the South. If you consider the staples of the South—rice and corn—and imagine them folded into a thick waffle batter, baked, and served with the region's famous Smithfield ham, mounded with a hearty stew, or served as an accompaniment to any dish with a rich gravy, you can understand the lasting appeal of a dinner waffle. ❡ In fact, the appeal has lasted, and even become trendy: Today, chefs across the country are putting waffles on their dinner menus. I wasn't at all surprised when my friend John Bennett, a well-known chef in Oklahoma City, made sour cream waffles topped with foie gras and chunky apple-rhubarb compote a signature dish, nor when New York restaurant critic and radio talk show host Arthur Schwartz pronounced waffles the new rage. ❡ These days I think of waffles the same way I think of potatoes, rice, barley, pasta, or bread—the perfect base for a saucy savory or the ideal side dish. And it was with these ideas in mind that I developed this collection of dinner waffles. Some of the waffles in this chapter are meant to be the main event, some the perfect accompaniment, and some, interchangeable. For example, Polenta Waffles with Creamy Goat Cheese Sauce could just as aptly be the side dish for a grilled steak dinner as the main course when the menu includes soup and salad. ❡ I've given you serving suggestions for each waffle, noted whether I thought it should be offered in a starring or supporting role, and recommended some variations, but I encourage you to do what I always do—play around. Try some of your regular pasta sauces, gravies, or flavored oils over the Mashed Potato Waffles; experiment with a vegetable stir-fry on top of the Parmesan-Walnut Waffles; or pull out all the stops and use the Creamed Spinach and Rice Waffles as the base for a mixed shellfish sauté. Dinner waffles are endlessly versatile, and if you follow my directions for making the waffles and then add your own toppings, you, too, will have a signature dish, a dish you can call your own.

Mashed Potato Waffles with
Garlic-Rosemary Oil

This recipe starts with silky mashed potatoes and ends with something even more sensational—mashed potatoes crisped in the waffle iron. The waffles are tender, almost fragile, and the insides are soft and well seasoned, much like a knish or a pirogi. Anything that tastes good over mashed potatoes—gravy, tomato sauce, sautéed mushrooms, the juice from a roasted chicken—is terrific over these waffles, but I encourage you to try them with a few spoonfuls of Garlic-Rosemary Oil.

PLAN AHEAD: The Garlic-Rosemary Oil is best made before you start the waffles.

The Waffles

2 russet potatoes (total weight about 1¼ pounds)
¼ cup extra-virgin olive oil
1 small onion, peeled and finely chopped
⅔ cup milk

Salt and freshly ground black pepper to taste
2 large eggs
1 cup all-purpose flour
2 teaspoons double-acting baking powder

MAKES ABOUT SIX 6½-INCH ROUND WAFFLES

❶ Peel and wash the potatoes. Cut them into small, evenly sized pieces, and put them in a large pot of cold, well-salted water; bring to the boil. Lower the heat and cook until you can pierce the potatoes easily with a fork. Drain and reserve about ½ cup of the potato water. Transfer the potatoes to a large mixing bowl.

❷ Heat the olive oil in a small skillet over low heat and sauté the chopped onion just until it softens a bit. Pour the oil and onion over the potatoes, then add the milk to the still-warm skillet—just to take the chill off it. Pour the milk over the potatoes.

❸ Mash the potatoes with the oil and milk. Add ¼ cup of the warm potato water, reserving the rest, and continue to mash until the mixture is smooth and looser than

continued

137

mashed potatoes you'd serve as a side dish. If it seems stiff, add more potato water, little by little, until you reach the desired consistency. Taste and season liberally with salt and pepper.

❹ Preheat your waffle iron. If you want to hold the finished waffles until serving time, preheat your oven to 200°F.

❺ Finish the batter by beating the eggs into the potatoes. Whisk together the flour and baking powder and fold them into the potatoes with a rubber spatula.

❻ Lightly butter or spray the grids of your waffle iron, if needed. Brush or spray the grids again only if subsequent waffles stick.

❼ Spoon out ½ cup of batter (or the amount recommended by your waffler's manufacturer) onto the hot iron. Smooth the batter evenly almost to the edge of the grids with a metal spatula or wooden spoon. Close the lid and bake until brown and crisp. Serve the waffles immediately or keep them, in a single layer, on a rack in the oven while you make the rest of the batch.

Topping: Garlic-Rosemary Oil

Flavored oils of every variety have sparked the imaginations of chefs across the country who use them to dress everything from simple salads to sliced fruits. Made by steeping herbs or spices in warm oil, these condiments are easy to make and extremely versatile. In this recipe, olive oil is infused with garlic and rosemary, ingredients with assertive flavors. The result is a marvelous match for these waffles.

3 large plump garlic cloves, peeled	One 4-inch sprig fresh rosemary or 1 teaspoon dried
½ cup virgin olive oil	½ teaspoon salt

Cut the garlic into very thin slices. Pour the oil into a small heavy skillet, add the sliced garlic and the rosemary, crushing the herb between your fingers as you add it to the skillet, and warm over low heat. When the garlic just starts to take on color (it should not brown), after about 5 to 7 minutes, remove the skillet from the heat. Add the salt and pour the oil through a fine strainer into a small pitcher. The oil is ready to use; it is delicious warm or at room temperature. (The oil can be made up to 2 weeks ahead, cooled to room temperature, poured into a jar with a tight-fitting lid, and stored in the refrigerator. Bring it to room temperature before using.)

SERVING: Serve these waffles in place of the potatoes you might ordinarily serve with grilled fish (salmon is swell with these) or simply roasted chicken or meat. For a light supper, serve the waffles with soup and a salad. Any leftover oil can be used to enliven steamed vegetables or grilled seafood. And, for a change, try these waffles topped with Basil-Garlic Sauce (page 155), another sharply seasoned sauce.

Spicy Ricotta Waffles with Grilled Pepper Strips

What gives these waffles their spicy heat is a generous amount of freshly ground black pepper. When baked through, they remain pale golden, their interior sponge light and creamy, very much like the ricotta cheese that forms their base. These are stunning made in a Belgian waffler, cut diagonally into triangles, and topped with grilled red peppers tossed in olive oil.

PLAN AHEAD: You can prepare the Grilled Pepper Strips up to 1 day before the waffles.

The Waffles

4 tablespoons (½ stick) unsalted butter	1 cup part-skim milk ricotta cheese
1¾ cups all-purpose flour	2 large eggs
2½ teaspoons double-acting baking powder	1¼ cups milk
½ teaspoon baking soda	
½ teaspoon salt	Fresh basil leaves for garnish
¾ teaspoon freshly ground black pepper	

MAKES ABOUT EIGHT 4½-INCH SQUARE BELGIAN WAFFLES

❶ Preheat your waffle iron. Preheat your oven to 200°F so you can hold the finished waffles until serving time.

❷ Melt the butter; reserve. In a medium-size bowl, whisk together the flour, baking powder, baking soda, salt, and pepper to combine. In a large bowl, beat the ricotta for 1 minute with a mixer until the mixer leaves tracks. Don't worry if it's not completely smooth. Add the eggs and beat for another minute. When the combination is smooth and shiny, add the milk. Turn the dry ingredients into the bowl with the ricotta mixture and whisk gently to combine. Stir in the melted butter.

❸ Lightly butter or spray the grids of your waffle iron, if needed. Brush or spray the grids again only if subsequent waffles stick.

❹ Spoon out 1 cup of batter for a Belgian waffler (or the amount recommended by your waffler's manufacturer) onto the hot iron. Spread the batter evenly over the grids with a metal spatula or wooden spoon, stopping right before the edge. Close the lid and bake until pale golden and lightly crisped. Put finished waffles in a single layer on a baking sheet, cover loosely with aluminum foil, and keep in the preheated oven while you make the rest of the batch.

Topping: Grilled Pepper Strips

When red bell peppers are grilled, peeled, and cut into thin strips as they are in this topping, they develop a sensuous, slippery texture and an extraordinary sweetness. Seasoned with coarse salt and freshly ground pepper, and bathed with extra-virgin olive oil, which seems to varnish their vivid color, these peppers are in gorgeous contrast to the pale, spicy waffles.

6 firm sweet red bell peppers	1 to 2 large plump garlic
¾ cup extra-virgin olive oil	cloves, peeled and very finely
Coarse salt and freshly ground	sliced (optional)
black pepper to taste	¼ cup fresh basil leaves

❶ The peppers need to be charred and peeled, a job an outdoor grill does well (grilling also adds its own wonderful flavor), but you can make fast work of these using your stove top. Work with one pepper at a time, impaling it on the tines of a long-handled fork and holding it over a gas flame or placing it directly on the heating element of an electric range. Turn the pepper often to char the skin deeply and evenly. Place the pepper in a paper bag, close the bag, and char the rest of the peppers. Allow the peppers to steam in the bag for about 10 minutes. When the peppers are cool enough to handle, remove and discard the charred skin, cut the peppers in half, and seed them. Slice the peppers lengthwise into strips, place them in a medium-size bowl, and toss with the olive oil and salt and pepper. Stir in the garlic, if you've chosen to use it, and taste, adding more salt or pepper if needed.

❷ At serving time, cut the basil into long strips and stir it into the pepper mixture.

SERVING: If your waffles are square, cut them diagonally to form triangles. If your waffles are another shape, serve them whole or cut them into shapes that please you. Top each piece with a layer of peppers and garnish each plate with a cluster of basil leaves. If you've prepared a salad (a leafy green salad is nice with these) or a green vegetable (such as crisp-cooked broccoli or string beans sprinkled with diced red onions), I recommend you offer them as side dishes.

New England Clam-Hash Waffles

I was introduced to clam hash years ago at Pat's Kountry Kitchen in Old Saybrook, Connecticut. Pat started the Kountry Kitchen as a six-table luncheonette and now presides over a large, full-service restaurant where, as before, the favorite dish is her clam hash. The hash is routinely praised in regional newspapers and magazines, but the recipe has never appeared in print—Pat won't part with it. (I tried to pry the recipe from her for an article I wrote for The New York Times—*no luck.) These waffles are my offbeat homage to Pat's local legend. They are thick, piquantly spiced, bursting with clams, and made with classic hash ingredients: potatoes and onions cooked in bacon drippings. They are the satisfying, down-to-earth stuff of an elbows-on-the-table supper. I suggest you enjoy these just the way people enjoy hash at Pat's, with a poached egg on top, coleslaw on the side, and some bottles of ketchup, Worcestershire, and Tabasco close by.*

1 potato (about ½ pound), peeled and cut into ¼-inch dice
3 strips bacon
3 tablespoons unsalted butter
1 large onion, peeled and finely chopped
15 ounces (one and one half 10-ounce cans) whole clams (or enough fresh clams to make 1½ cups), drained
1 teaspoon fresh thyme, chopped, or ¼ teaspoon dried
Salt and freshly ground black pepper to taste

1 cup all-purpose flour
2 teaspoons double-acting baking powder
1 cup bottled clam juice
2 large eggs
Tabasco to taste
Worcestershire sauce to taste
1 tablespoon finely chopped fresh parsley

Poached eggs, coleslaw, and ketchup as accompaniments (optional)

MAKES ABOUT SEVEN 4½-INCH SQUARE BELGIAN WAFFLES

❶ Steam the potato cubes until they can be pierced easily with a knife, 10 to 15 minutes. Drain and, when cool enough to handle, pat dry between paper towels; set aside.

❷ Lay the bacon strips in a large skillet, preferably nonstick, and cook over medium heat until browned on the underside. Turn the strips and cook until evenly browned on the other side; remove from the heat. You'll be using the bacon fat, so don't discard it. Transfer the bacon to a double thickness of paper towels to drain. When cool enough to handle, crumble the bacon and set aside.

❸ Return the skillet to medium heat and add the butter; heat until the butter and bacon fat are foamy. Add the chopped onion and cook, stirring, until the onion softens and starts to turn golden. Add the reserved potato cubes and continue to stir just long enough to warm the potatoes and coat them with the cooking fats. Add the clams, thyme, and reserved bacon. Stir and season well with salt and pepper, remembering that you'll be adding Tabasco and Worcestershire sauce.

❹ Preheat your waffle iron. If you want to hold the finished waffles until serving time, preheat your oven to 200°F.

❺ In a large bowl, whisk together the flour and baking powder. In another bowl, whisk together the clam juice and eggs until very well mixed. Add the liquid ingredients to the dry ingredients and whisk until just combined. Stir in the reserved clam mixture. Season with Tabasco and Worcestershire sauce and fold in the parsley.

❻ Lightly butter or spray the grids of your waffle iron, if needed. Brush or spray the grids again only if subsequent waffles stick.

❼ Spoon out 1 cup of batter for a Belgian waffler (or the amount recommended by your waffler's manufacturer) onto the grids, using a metal spatula or wooden spoon to spread the mixture evenly across the grids. Close the lid and bake until golden and lightly crisped. Serve the waffles immediately or keep them, in a single layer, on a rack in the preheated oven while you make the rest of the batch. Before measuring out the batter for each waffle, remember to stir the mixture.

SERVING: Since each waffle weighs about ¼ pound, you might want to serve just one per person. Put the waffles on warm plates and serve with "the works"—a poached egg, a selection of condiments including ketchup, and some freshly made coleslaw. As you'd expect, these are just the thing with very cold beer. But you can turn them into a company offering by forgoing the poached egg and replacing the ketchup with a warm, spicy tomato sauce or a room-temperature salsa of diced red peppers, juicy ripe tomatoes, onions, and olive oil. Exchange the coleslaw for a crisp green salad and you've got a dinner that commands candles and wine.

Halloween Waffles

No one will say "boo" if you serve these waffles often in the fall. They're jam-packed with the foods of a fall cornucopia and the colors of a Halloween landscape: red apples, orange acorn squash, yellow cornmeal, and russet cider, maple syrup, and spices. Because the acorn squash is shredded, there's no need to cook it ahead of time; the heat of the waffle iron bakes and mellows it.

4 tablespoons (½ stick) unsalted butter

6 ounces acorn squash (about ½ small squash), peeled and seeded

1 medium McIntosh apple

⅓ cup pecans, coarsely chopped

1¼ cups all-purpose flour

½ cup yellow cornmeal

1 tablespoon double-acting baking powder

⅛ teaspoon salt

¼ teaspoon ground cinnamon

⅛ teaspoon ground cloves

1¼ cups apple cider

2 tablespoons pure maple syrup

2 large eggs

Maple syrup, applesauce, pumpkin butter, or maple butter for topping (optional)

MAKES ABOUT FIVE 6½-INCH ROUND WAFFLES

❶ Preheat your waffle iron. If you want to hold the finished waffles until serving time, preheat your oven to 200°F.

❷ Melt the butter; reserve. Use the large-holed side of a box grater to grate the acorn squash. You should have 1¼ packed cups of shredded squash. Place the squash in a bowl. Peel and core the apple; cut it into small dice and add it to the bowl with the squash. Add the pecans, stir to mix, and set aside.

❸ In a large bowl, whisk together the flour, cornmeal, baking powder, salt, cinnamon, and cloves. In another bowl, whisk together the cider, syrup, and eggs until very well mixed. Pour the liquid ingredients over the dry ingredients and stir with a whisk until just combined. Stir in the squash, apple, and pecans and fold in the melted butter.

❹ Lightly butter or spray the grids of your waffle iron, if needed. Brush or spray the grids again only if subsequent waffles stick.

❺ Spoon out a scant 1 cup of batter (or more than the amount your waffler's manufacturer recommends) onto the grids. Use a metal spatula or wooden spoon to spread the chunky batter evenly across the grids. Close the lid and bake until golden. If you are not serving the waffles immediately, put them in a single layer on a baking sheet, loosely covered with aluminum foil, in the preheated oven while you make the rest of the batch.

SERVING: Serve these topped with pure maple syrup or Rosy Applesauce (page 101) alongside game or a roast, or as a main course with a large chunk of sharp-flavored cheese, such as aged Gruyère, and a side serving of a lightly dressed green vegetable. It wouldn't be too much to top these with a pat of maple butter or a dollop of first-quality store-bought pumpkin butter. Since fall fruits and vegetables lend themselves to such lovely variations, you might want to experiment with other mixtures. For example, try combining pumpkin, pears, walnuts, and orange zest, or other mixtures inspired by what's available at the green market.

Cranberry Waffles with
Cranberry-Orange Relish

Fresh cranberries are the harbinger of the holiday season and here they are used two ways: The puckery-tart berries are folded into soft yogurt waffles and cooked with orange to make a sparkling relish. These are worthy of accompanying the Thanksgiving turkey to the table.

PLAN AHEAD: The relish can be made up to 2 weeks ahead and kept covered and refrigerated.

The Waffles

3 tablespoons unsalted butter
1¼ cups all-purpose flour
2 teaspoons double-acting
　baking powder
¼ teaspoon baking soda
½ teaspoon ground ginger
¼ cup sugar
¾ cup fresh orange juice
½ cup plain yogurt

2 large eggs
1 cup fresh or frozen
　cranberries, chopped (if
　frozen, *don't* thaw before
　using)
⅓ cup walnuts, coarsely
　chopped
Grated zest of 1 orange

MAKES ABOUT FIVE 6½-INCH ROUND WAFFLES

❶ Preheat your waffle iron. If you want to hold the finished waffles until serving time, preheat your oven to 200°F.

❷ Melt the butter; reserve. In a large bowl, whisk together the flour, baking powder, baking soda, ginger, and sugar. In another bowl, whisk together the orange juice, yogurt, and eggs until very well blended. Pour the liquid ingredients over the dry ingredients and whisk until just combined. Stir in the cranberries, walnuts, and rind. When blended, stir in the melted butter.

❸ Lightly butter or spray the grids of your waffle iron, if needed. Brush or spray the grids again only if subsequent waffles stick.

❹ Spoon out ⅔ cup of batter (or slightly more than your waffler's manufacturer suggests) onto the grids. Spread it evenly up to the edge of the iron with a metal spatula or wooden spoon. Close the lid and bake the waffle until lightly browned and set. If you're not going to serve the waffles immediately, put them in a single layer on a baking sheet, cover them loosely with aluminum foil, and keep them in the pre-heated oven while you make the rest of the batch.

Topping: Cranberry-Orange Relish

Glistening, sprightly, and surprisingly simple to make, this relish is one you'll want to serve often over Cranberry Waffles or alongside poultry. It is a tart relish, cooked just until the berries pop and start to gel, and then finished with a few spoonfuls of orange marmalade, an unexpected addition that lends another zesty note to the mixture. Since cranberries are in the market only a short time but will keep in the freezer for 1 year, it's always a good idea to stock up when you find them.

2 cups cranberries, fresh or
    frozen (if they're frozen, *don't*
    defrost them)
1 cup fresh orange juice

½ cup sugar
2 tablespoons first-quality
    orange marmalade

Put the cranberries, orange juice, and sugar in a heavy-bottomed saucepan and stir with a wooden spoon to mix. Place the pan over medium-high heat and bring to the boil. Lower the heat and cook, stirring often, until the berries pop and the mixture thickens, about 5 to 8 minutes. (Don't walk away from the pot; the relish can burn in a flash.) Stir in the marmalade and cook, stirring constantly, for another 1 to 2 minutes. Remove from the heat and cool to room temperature. Don't worry if the relish isn't thick when you pull the pot off the stove; it will thicken as it cools.

SERVING: Cut the waffles into quarters and serve with a spoonful of relish on each quarter, or divvy up the relish and allow each person to dip as desired. While a natural with poultry and game, these lively relish-topped waffles are fabulous with grilled fish. Try them with a meaty fish like swordfish or a mild fish like cod.

Double Wild: Wild Rice Waffles
with Wild Mushroom Sauce

This is consummate cold-weather food: hearty waffles chockablock with nutty wild rice, browned onions, garlic, and herbs, topped with a creamy, mouthwatering mixture of mushrooms. Wild rice is not a true grain; it is a type of grass native to America that cooks to a firm, chewy finish and captures in each brown and white morsel myriad earthy flavors. The taste is complex and in these waffles it is deepened by the addition of herbs, both subtle and strong, and a mixture of chicken broth and tangy buttermilk. While these Wild Rice Waffles are substantial, they are also refined, delicately balanced, and elegant, an entrée equally at ease at a dressy dinner or casual supper.

PLAN AHEAD: Make the waffles in advance and reheat them while you're making the sauce.

The Waffles

¼ cup virgin olive oil

2 onions, peeled and finely chopped

2 large plump garlic cloves, peeled and finely chopped

1 teaspoon salt

½ teaspoon freshly ground black pepper

¾ teaspoon herbes de Provence or ¼ teaspoon dried thyme

2 cups cooked wild rice

¼ cup packed fresh parsley, minced

2 tablespoons snipped fresh chives

1¼ cups all-purpose flour

2 teaspoons double-acting baking powder

¼ teaspoon baking soda

1 cup chicken broth

¼ cup buttermilk

2 large eggs

MAKES SIX 4½-INCH SQUARE BELGIAN WAFFLES

❶ Preheat your waffle iron.

❷ Heat the olive oil in a large skillet, preferably nonstick, over medium-high heat. Add the onions and cook, stirring, until lightly browned. Add the garlic, salt, pepper, and herbes de Provence and continue to cook for 1 minute more. Add the wild rice and stir just until the mixture is well combined. Off heat, mix in the parsley and chives. The rice mixture should be well seasoned, so taste it and adjust the salt, pepper, and herbs as needed. Reserve.

❸ In a large bowl, whisk together the flour, baking powder, and baking soda. In another bowl, beat together the chicken broth, buttermilk, and eggs with a whisk. Pour the liquid ingredients over the dry ingredients and stir together with the whisk until just combined. Stir in the wild rice mixture.

❹ Lightly butter or spray the grids of your waffle iron, if needed. Brush or spray the grids again only if subsequent waffles stick.

❺ Spoon out 1 cup of batter for a Belgian waffler (or the measure recommended by your waffler's manufacturer) onto the hot iron. This batter is thick and won't budge, so use a metal spatula or wooden spoon to spread it evenly across the grids. Close the lid and bake until the waffle is golden and crisp. Because the waffle is thick, it's a good idea to turn it midway through its baking time. Put the finished waffles on a cooling rack while you make the rest of the batch and the topping. When you're ready to make the sauce, put the waffles in a single layer on a baking sheet, cover them loosely with aluminum foil, and reheat in a preheated 350°F oven for about 5 to 10 minutes.

Topping: Wild Mushroom Sauce

This sauce has the creamy richness and tang you expect from heavy cream, but it's made with nonfat sour cream thinned with low-fat buttermilk. Try this combination when you're making a pasta sauce or looking for something special for sautéed scallops or mixed vegetables.

3 tablespoons extra-virgin olive oil
1 onion, peeled and finely chopped
Salt and freshly ground black pepper to taste
¾ pound assorted fresh wild mushrooms, such as cremini, shiitake, oyster, and chanterelle, cleaned, trimmed, and thinly sliced

½ cup Madeira or dry sherry
½ cup nonfat sour cream
1 cup buttermilk
6 scallions, white part only, thinly sliced
2 tablespoons snipped fresh dill

continued

Heat the olive oil in a large skillet over medium-high heat. Add the onion, salt, and pepper and sauté until the onion softens and starts to brown. Add the mushrooms and cook until softened. Pour over the Madeira and cook, stirring, until the liquid is almost evaporated. Mix together the sour cream and buttermilk and add to the skillet. Bring to the boil, stirring; lower the heat and simmer for 2 minutes. The mixture will thicken slightly and be ivory-colored. Stir in the scallions and dill, adjust the seasonings, and serve immediately.

SERVING: Place one waffle on each warm dinner plate and ladle over a generous portion of sauce. For an easy, gracious dinner, start with a light, clear soup, present Double Wild Waffles as the main course, follow with a salad of romaine, endive, and walnuts, and serve a fruity dessert. A chilled, very dry white wine is the right companion for this rich dish.

Creamed Spinach and Rice Waffles
with Sautéed Scallops

Save these rich waffles topped with quickly sautéed bay scallops for an evening when you're entertaining lavishly. The rice is not immediately distinguishable at first bite, but it is the grain that gives these waffles their singular texture and makes them a superb base for scallops finished with a savory wine and tomato sauce.

PLAN AHEAD: Make the waffles ahead and reheat them while you are finishing the Sautéed Scallops.

The Waffles

10 ounces fresh spinach, trimmed and washed
1½ cups all-purpose flour
1 tablespoon double-acting baking powder
1 teaspoon salt
¾ teaspoon freshly ground black pepper

1¼ cups chicken broth
½ cup heavy cream
2 large eggs
2 large plump garlic cloves, pressed
¾ cup cooked white rice
¼ cup extra-virgin olive oil

MAKES ABOUT EIGHT 4½-INCH SQUARE BELGIAN WAFFLES

❶ Drain most of the water from the washed spinach. Place the spinach in a large skillet over medium heat. Cover and cook in the water that clings to the leaves, stirring frequently, until the spinach is wilted, about 5 minutes. Put into a colander and, when it is cool enough to handle, press the spinach between your palms to rid it of as much water as possible. Separate the leaves as best you can and set aside.

❷ Preheat your waffle iron.

❸ In a large bowl, whisk together the flour, baking powder, salt, and pepper to mix. In another bowl, whisk together the broth, cream, eggs, and garlic until well blended. Pour the liquid ingredients over the dry ingredients and stir with the whisk until the mixtures are just combined. Fold in the spinach, rice, and olive oil.

continued

❹ Lightly butter or spray the grids of your waffle iron, if needed. Brush or spray the grids again only if subsequent waffles stick.

❺ Spoon out 1 cup of batter for the Belgian waffler (or the measure recommended by your waffler's manufacturer) onto the iron and use a metal spatula or wooden spoon to spread it evenly across the grids. Close the lid and bake until the waffle is golden brown, turning it over midway through the baking to even the color. Keep finished waffles, in a single layer, on a cooling rack while you prepare the scallops.

❻ When you are ready to serve the waffles, preheat your oven to 350°F. Place the waffles in a single layer on a baking sheet, cover loosely with a sheet of aluminum foil, and bake until heated through, about 8 to 10 minutes.

Topping: Sautéed Scallops

This is an easy, thoroughly luscious way to prepare scallops. If it is not possible to find small bay scallops, you can buy larger sea scallops and cut each scallop into quarters. Whether you buy bay or sea scallops, it is important that they be pristinely fresh. A perfect scallop is firm, shiny, and smells sweetly of the sea.

2 pounds bay scallops, small muscle removed
Salt and freshly ground black pepper to taste
¼ cup extra-virgin olive oil
2 large shallots, peeled and finely minced
2 large plump garlic cloves, peeled and pressed
½ cup white wine or dry white vermouth

1 cup chicken broth or bottled clam juice
1 cup heavy cream
2 tablespoons tomato paste
2 large tomatoes, peeled, seeded, and finely diced
1 tablespoon minced fresh parsley or snipped fresh chives

❶ Rinse the scallops and pat dry between paper towels. Toss with salt and pepper to season well; set aside.

❷ Heat the olive oil in a large skillet over medium heat. Add the shallots and sauté just until they are covered with oil. Raise the heat to medium-high and add the scallops. Sauté for 60 to 90 seconds, just until the scallops firm and start to take on the lightest color. Remove the skillet from the heat and lift the scallops out with a slotted spoon, setting them aside in a bowl while you make the sauce.

❸ Return the skillet to medium-high heat, add the garlic, and sauté, stirring constantly, for 1 minute. Add the wine and chicken broth and stir to scrape up any browned bits clinging to the bottom of the pan. Cook until the liquid is reduced by half, about 5 minutes. Whisk in the heavy cream, tomato paste, and any liquid that has accumulated in the bowl with the scallops. Boil for 2 to 3 minutes more, or until the sauce thickens slightly. Reduce the heat to medium. Return the scallops to the pan along with the tomatoes. Cook for 30 seconds more. Taste the sauce and add more salt and pepper as needed. Remove from the heat, stir in the parsley or chives, and serve immediately.

SERVING: Cut the hot waffles in half diagonally and place the pieces, slightly overlapping, on warm dinner plates. Spoon over the scallops and sauce and serve immediately. I don't like to serve anything else on the dinner plates with these waffles—they are a full meal of vegetable, grain, and fish.

Parmesan-Walnut Waffles
with Basil-Garlic Sauce

Sharp flavored, beautifully crumbly Parmesan cheese is a culinary treasure. Delicious eaten solo, it is superb mixed with walnuts to make tender waffles topped with Basil-Garlic Sauce. The next time you're thinking of pasta for supper, turn to these instead.

PLAN AHEAD: The Basil-Garlic Sauce is best made before you start the waffles.

The Waffles

1½ cups all-purpose flour
2 teaspoons double-acting
   baking powder
½ teaspoon salt
1½ cups milk

2 large eggs
¾ cup freshly grated Parmesan
   cheese
⅓ cup coarsely chopped
   walnuts
¼ cup extra-virgin olive oil

MAKES ABOUT FIVE 6½-INCH ROUND WAFFLES

❶ Preheat your waffle iron. If you want to hold the finished waffles until serving time, preheat your oven to 200°F.

❷ In a large bowl, whisk together the flour, baking powder, and salt to mix. In another bowl, whisk together the milk and eggs to blend very well. Pour the liquid ingredients over the dry ingredients and whisk until just combined. Fold in the Parmesan cheese and walnuts, then the olive oil.

❸ Lightly butter or spray the grids of your waffle iron, if needed. Brush or spray the grids again only if subsequent waffles stick.

❹ Spoon out ½ cup of batter (or the amount recommended by your waffler's manufacturer) onto the grids. Spread the batter evenly over the grids with a metal spatula or wooden spoon. Close the lid and bake until the waffle is browned and set. Serve the waffles immediately or keep them, in a single layer, on a rack in the preheated oven while you make the rest of the batch.

Topping: Basil-Garlic Sauce

The ingredients for this pestolike sauce are simple—fresh basil, a few garlic cloves, salt, and fine olive oil—but without pesto's traditional additions of Parmesan, nuts, pasta water, and butter to tamp down the tastes, the strong, clear flavors of the basil and garlic are free to sing out. This is a gutsy sauce that pleases garlic's most passionate lovers.

2 cups packed fresh basil, trimmed, washed, and very well dried (if fresh basil is out of season, substitute an equal amount of trimmed fresh spinach)

1 teaspoon salt (or more to taste)
2 large plump garlic cloves, peeled and sliced
¾ cup extra-virgin olive oil

Put all the ingredients in the workbowl of a food processor or a blender and process until smooth, scraping down the sides as needed. (The sauce can be made up to 1 week in advance, covered tightly, and stored in the refrigerator; it can be frozen for up to 2 months.)

SERVING: Cut the waffles into quarters, spoon over some of the Basil-Garlic Sauce, and serve as an accompaniment to roast chicken, grilled chops, stews, or sautéed seafood. Leftover waffles are delicious with tomato sauce; leftover sauce can be used over pasta, rice, potatoes, or grilled fish.

Apple, Onion, and Gruyère Waffles

A French friend of mine always won raves when she made a soft, dinner-size omelet filled with slices of Golden Delicious apples, yellow onions, and Gruyère, a nutty-flavored, semihard cheese with marvelous meltability. Happily, this thoroughly appealing filling translates flawlessly to waffles. The batter turns out waffles that are thick and cakey with a fine sweet-tangy balance. As for an accompaniment, you can take your pick, choosing to play up the sweet flavors with a layer of homemade applesauce (page 101), the tart with a blanket of yogurt, or the middle ground with Lightly Pickled Onions.

PLAN AHEAD: **Prepare the Lightly Pickled Onions before you start the waffles.**

The Waffles

4 tablespoons (½ stick) unsalted butter
1 cup all-purpose flour
½ cup whole-wheat flour
1 tablespoon double-acting baking powder
¼ teaspoon baking soda
¼ teaspoon salt
¼ teaspoon freshly ground black pepper

1¾ cups buttermilk
2 large eggs
1 Golden Delicious apple, peeled, cored, and thinly sliced
1 small onion, peeled, halved, and thinly sliced
½ cup grated Gruyère or Swiss cheese

MAKES ABOUT FIVE 6½-INCH ROUND WAFFLES

❶ Preheat your waffle iron. If you want to hold the finished waffles until serving time, preheat your oven to 200°F.

❷ Melt the butter; reserve. In a large bowl, whisk together the flours, baking powder, baking soda, salt, and pepper until mixed. In another bowl, whisk together the buttermilk and eggs until very well blended. Pour the liquid ingredients over the dry ingredients and whisk to combine. Fold in the apple, onion, and Gruyère, then the melted butter.

❸ Lightly butter or spray the grids of your waffle iron, if needed. Brush or spray the grids again only if subsequent waffles stick.

❹ Spoon out ½ cup of batter (or the amount recommended by your waffler's manu-facturer) onto the grids. Use a metal spatula or wooden spoon to spread the thick, lumpy batter over the grids. Close the lid and bake until golden brown. Serve the waffles immediately or keep them, in a single layer, on a rack in the preheated oven while you make the rest of the batch.

Topping: Lightly Pickled Onions

This is a delightful, refreshing salad with a slight crunch, a mildly vinegary flavor, and just enough sugar to tie it together with the tastes of the waffles it tops.

3 medium onions, peeled
1 cup cider vinegar
½ cup water
2 tablespoons sugar (or more to taste)

1½ teaspoons salt
Chopped fresh parsley
   (optional)

Cut the onions in half from top to bottom. Working with the flat, cut side of the onion down, slice the onions into paper-thin slices. Put the onions in a nonreactive bowl, separating the pieces as you do. Add the remaining ingredients, *except* the parsley, and stir well. Cover with plastic wrap and set aside until needed. (The salad can be made several hours or up to 1 day in advance, and kept covered and refrigerated.) Just before serving, drain the onions, reserving the marinade, and stir in the chopped parsley. (Stir the reserved marinade into any leftover onions and refrigerate.)

SERVING: Serve hot quartered waffles as a side dish, placing a generous portion of Lightly Pickled Onions next to each waffle. These waffles are delicious with grilled seafood or chicken and robust enough to stand in as the main course for an informal supper. Just fill out the menu with a crisp salad (spinach salad with bacon is an outstanding choice) and a not-too-heavy dessert such as chocolate sorbet or crunchy sugar cookies with fruit.

Polenta Waffles

with Creamy Goat Cheese Sauce

Because polenta is now so popular, it's easy to think of it as a trendy dish rather than a classic with a rich history. Like mamaliga from Romania or grits from America's South, polenta is an elemental mixture of corn and water, patiently stirred until it is thick and satiny. If you've already tried Crispy Cornmeal Waffles (page 44) or Cilantro Waffle Chips (page 113), you'll be astonished at how different polenta waffles are from others made with cornmeal: They are fluffy, finely textured, and subtle. These straddle the line between peasant and posh; serve them with Creamy Goat Cheese Sauce and they'll be unmistakably sophisticated.

PLAN AHEAD: You can make the Creamy Goat Cheese Sauce before you make the waffles, keeping the sauce warm in a double boiler, or you can prepare the waffles ahead and reheat them once the sauce is made.

The Waffles

2 cups water
1 teaspoon coarse salt
4 tablespoons (½ stick)
  unsalted butter, cut into 4
  pieces
⅓ cup coarse cornmeal
  (preferably a stone-ground
  brand)

2 large eggs
½ cup all-purpose flour
1 teaspoon double-acting
  baking powder

MAKES ABOUT FOUR 6½-INCH ROUND WAFFLES

❶ To make the polenta, heat the water, salt, and butter in a 2-quart saucepan over medium-high heat. When the water has come to the boil and the butter is melted or almost completely melted, reduce the heat to low and very slowly and very gradually add the cornmeal to the pan, stirring constantly with a wooden spoon. It is important not to let the cornmeal form lumps, and the best way to do this is to add the cornmeal in a trickle and stir vigorously and without stop. When all the cornmeal has been added, continue to stir over low heat until the mixture is thick, smooth, and shiny, about 15 minutes. Your spoon will leave tracks and the polenta will be almost thick enough to mound on a spoon but thin enough to pour or spread. Pour the polenta into a large bowl.

❷ Preheat your waffle iron. If you want to hold the waffles until serving time, pre-heat your oven to 200°F.

❸ One at a time, beat the eggs into the polenta with a whisk. In a small bowl, whisk together the flour and baking powder just to combine, then turn this mixture out over the polenta. Fold the dry ingredients into the polenta.

❹ Lightly butter or spray the grids of your iron, if needed. Brush or spray the grids again only if subsequent waffles stick.

❺ Spoon out ½ cup of batter (or the amount recommended by your waffler's manu-facturer) onto the hot grids. Spread the batter evenly across the grids with a metal spatula or wooden spoon. Close the lid and bake until the waffle is honey brown and set. Serve the waffles immediately or keep them, in a single layer, on a rack in the preheated oven while you make the rest of the batch.

Topping: Creamy Goat Cheese Sauce

This warm, tangy mixture of soft goat cheese, melted and thinned with milk, is excellent without adornment.

6 ounces fresh soft goat cheese	Herbes de Provence to taste
¾ cup milk	(optional)
Salt and white pepper to taste	

Put the goat cheese and milk in the top of a double boiler placed over simmering water; do not allow the bottom of the pot containing the cheese to touch the hot water. Cook over medium heat, stirring, until the cheese melts and the mixture is smooth. Be careful not to overcook; too much heat can curdle the mixture. Stir in the salt, pepper, and herbes de Provence, if wanted. The sauce is ready to serve as soon as the mixture is melted and creamy. (If you want to make the sauce ahead, remove it from the double boiler, cool, and refrigerate it, covered, until needed. Right before serving, reheat it in the double boiler.)

SERVING: The waffles can be served as a side dish to accompany chicken or fish, in which case you'll want to quarter the waffles and serve two or three pieces to each person. They also can be presented whole as a main dish with a vegetable and tossed salad on the side.

6

Finishers

Devilishly Delicious Dessert Waffles

Having been born with a sweet tooth, worked as a pastry chef, and written a dessert cookbook, I've tried to find an imperative for making dessert one of the necessary food groups—and failed. It is pure gustatory hedonism, and we love it for just that reason. ❡ In many ways I think we expect more of desserts than we do of any other type of food. That they must taste good is a given, but we add to that the demand that desserts make us feel pampered, pleased, and completely satisfied. For those of us who adore desserts and love waffles, it is no wonder that a sweet waffle can do this and more. ❡ Plain waffles can certainly pamper us. From their homey shapes and comforting scents (few things smell as enticing as warm butter and sugar) to their soft inner sponges and lightly crisped crusts, waffles are a food that delights every sense, even that of sound: The sizzle of batter on the hot grids is a call to enjoyment. But when waffles are enhanced by fruit, ice cream, spices, chocolate, or whipped cream—some of the adornments and additions they receive in this chapter—they become a sublime indulgence. ❡ In this chapter, I have created desserts that span the range of indulgences and stretch the limits of what many of us thought of as waffle desserts. Some of the desserts, like Double Vanilla Waffles, are as comforting as bread pudding, some, like Lemon Meringue Waffles, as sharply flavored and refreshing as sorbet, and others, like White Chocolate Chip Waffles, as soul-satisfying as a hot fudge sundae with "the works." ❡ The sweets here can be served after dinner or on their own, with a cup of espresso or a coupe of champagne, early in the evening or as the clock strikes midnight. These are desserts that will spoil you and your friends in the most delightful way.

Double Vanilla Waffles

These honey-brown, lightly crisp waffles show off vanilla's most treasured qualities—its dizzying aroma, warm, round flavor, and natural ability to bring out the best in other ingredients. Here, vanilla is used in two forms, bean and extract, and blended with dark brown "burnt" butter—butter that has been browned until its aroma resembles that of warmed hazelnuts. The toasty, nutty taste of the browned butter and the deep fragrance and flavor of vanilla are a sublime combination that makes a splendid waffle.
I suggest making these in a Belgian waffle iron with deep grids, the better to hold the vanilla-perfumed Pear Sauce, but they'd be just as wonderful made in any other kind of waffler.

PLAN AHEAD: **Make the Pear Sauce while the vanilla bean is steeping in the milk for the waffles.**

The Waffles

1¾ cups milk	Pinch of salt
½ large soft vanilla bean	⅓ cup sugar
5 tablespoons unsalted butter	2 large eggs
1¾ cups all-purpose flour	1 teaspoon pure vanilla extract
2 teaspoons double-acting	
baking powder	Vanilla ice cream (optional)

MAKES ABOUT EIGHT 4½-INCH SQUARE BELGIAN WAFFLES

❶ Pour the milk into a medium-size saucepan. Split the vanilla bean half lengthwise and scrape the soft inner pulp (the seeds) into the milk; add the pod. Bring the milk to the boil, remove from the heat, cover, and set aside to steep for at least 1 hour, allowing the vanilla to flavor the milk.

❷ Place the butter in a small skillet over medium heat. Cook until the butter melts, turns golden brown, and gives off a warm, nutty aroma. Take care not to let it burn. Set aside.

❸ Preheat your waffle iron. If you want to hold the finished waffles until serving time, preheat your oven to 200°F.

continued

❹ In a large bowl, whisk together the flour, baking powder, salt, and sugar to blend. Remove the vanilla bean pod from the milk and discard it, or rinse and dry it and use it to flavor sugar. Add the browned butter, eggs, and vanilla to the saucepan of milk; whisk to mix well. Pour the liquid ingredients over the dry ingredients and whisk until just combined.

❺ Lightly butter or spray the grids of your waffle iron, if needed. Brush or spray the grids again only if subsequent waffles stick.

❻ Spoon out ⅔ cup of batter for a Belgian waffler (or the amount recommended by your waffler's manufacturer) onto the hot iron. Smooth the batter evenly over the grids with a metal spatula or wooden spoon. Close the lid and bake until brown and crisp. Serve these immediately or keep them, in a single layer, on a rack in the preheated oven while you make the rest of the batch.

Topping: Pear Sauce

This sauce is as easy to make and enjoy as applesauce, but if you choose beautifully ripe pears and cook them slowly with a plump vanilla bean, you will create something celestial. Starting with perfect ingredients is everything with this sauce.

½ large soft vanilla bean	1 teaspoon fresh lemon juice
4 ripe juicy Comice, Bartlett, or	2 tablespoons water
Anjou pears, peeled and cut	1 to 2 tablespoons sugar or
into chunks	honey to taste

❶ Split the vanilla bean half lengthwise. Scrape the soft seeds from the bean into a medium-size saucepan and add the pod. Add the pears, lemon juice, and water to the saucepan and bring to a boil over medium heat. Cover the pan, reduce the heat to low, and cook until the pears can be mashed easily with the back of a spoon, about 20 minutes, adding more water, a tablespoon at a time, if needed. Remove the vanilla bean pod and discard or reserve it to flavor sugar.

❷ Pour the pears and their liquid into the workbowl of a food processor or a blender and process until the sauce is very smooth. Add sugar or honey to taste, then set aside to cool. Serve slightly warm, at room temperature, or chilled. (You can make the sauce ahead; cover and refrigerate for 1 week or freeze for 1 month.)

SERVING: The first time I made these waffles, they reminded me of pound cake. Because there's something as rich and satisfying about these waffles as there is about a finely made cake, I find myself craving these with tea as a late-afternoon treat. But they're certainly elegant enough for evening. Offer cups of steaming espresso and crown each waffle with a generous topping of Pear Sauce and vanilla-bean ice cream.

Gingerbread Ice-Cream Hearts

While your entire house will smell like Christmas when you make these waffles, you'll want to make them at all special times throughout the year. Their taste is as full-flavored as Britain's best gingerbread cake (thanks to a wonderful mix of spices, buttermilk, and molasses) and the perfect contrast for a frosty vanilla ice-cream filling. Don't dismiss these as snack food for kids; these hearts are sophisticated sweets deserving of your best china.

I make these in the five-of-hearts waffle iron, separating the five little hearts and pairing them to be filled with ice cream. If you want to make them in a regular waffle iron, make them thin and crisp. Use two waffles to make an ice-cream sandwich, then cut the large waffles into manageable squares.

4 tablespoons (½ stick)
 unsalted butter
2 cups all-purpose flour
1 tablespoon double-acting
 baking powder
¾ teaspoon baking soda
¼ teaspoon salt
1 tablespoon ground ginger
¾ teaspoon ground cinnamon
½ teaspoon dried mustard
¼ teaspoon ground cloves
¼ teaspoon freshly grated
 nutmeg

¾ cup firmly packed dark
 brown sugar
1½ cups buttermilk
¼ cup unsulfured molasses
2 large eggs, separated

1 quart vanilla ice cream,
 softened, to fill the
 sandwiches
Coarsely chopped crystallized
 ginger (optional)
Confectioners' sugar for
 dusting

MAKES ABOUT 8 FULL FIVE-OF-HEARTS WAFFLES
OR 20 SANDWICHES

❶ Preheat your waffle iron.

❷ Melt the butter; reserve. In a large bowl, whisk together the flour, baking powder, baking soda, salt, spices, and sugar to combine. In another bowl, whisk together the buttermilk, molasses, and egg yolks. In a clean dry bowl with a clean dry beater, whip the egg whites until they hold firm peaks. Blend the buttermilk mixture into the dry ingredients with a whisk, stirring just until the mixtures are combined. Stir in the melted butter, then gently fold in the egg whites.

❸ Lightly butter or spray the grids of your waffle iron, if needed. Brush or spray the grids again only if subsequent waffles stick.

❹ Spoon out ½ cup of batter (or the amount recommended by your waffler's manufacturer) onto the hot iron. Spread the batter evenly over the grids with a metal spatula or wooden spoon, stopping right before the edge. Close the lid and bake until deep brown and set. Cool the finished waffles in a single layer on a rack.

❺ When the waffles are at room temperature, cut them into hearts with scissors or a serrated knife and spread half of them evenly with softened ice cream to a thickness of about ¼ inch; top with the remaining hearts. If you want to decorate the sides of the sandwiches with crystallized ginger, press the ginger into the ice cream with your fingertips. Transfer the sandwiches to a waxed paper–lined baking sheet and freeze until firm. When firm, wrap the hearts in a double thickness of plastic wrap or aluminum foil. (They'll keep in the freezer for about 2 weeks.)

SERVING: Serve the hearts directly from the freezer. Place them on a beautiful serving platter or arrange them on individual dessert plates in the kitchen, allowing two to three sandwiches per person. Dust the tops lightly with confectioners' sugar.

Spiced Plum Waffles

These waffles are outstanding whether made with the red, black, or green plums that show up on the fruit stands early in the summer or the small, oval purple plums, sometimes called Italian or prune plums, that arrive in the fall and mark the end of the season. The lush blend of spices in the batter, including highly aromatic coriander, coupled with the waffle iron's heat, heighten the honeylike sweetness and soft texture that make perfectly ripe plums such a sensuous fruit.

PLAN AHEAD: Make the Orange-Plum Sauce and set it aside before you make the waffles.

The Waffles

5 tablespoons unsalted butter
2 cups all-purpose flour
1 tablespoon double-acting
   baking powder
½ teaspoon baking soda
Pinch of salt
1 teaspoon finely chopped or
   grated orange zest
½ teaspoon ground ginger
¼ teaspoon ground cinnamon
⅛ teaspoon ground coriander
⅓ cup firmly packed light
   brown sugar

1¼ cups milk
½ cup fresh orange juice
2 large eggs
½ teaspoon pure vanilla extract
¼ teaspoon pure almond
   extract
2 sweet ripe plums (about ½
   pound total), pitted and finely
   cubed

Ice cream or lightly sweetened
   whipped cream (optional)

MAKES ABOUT SIX 6½-INCH ROUND WAFFLES

❶ Preheat your waffle iron. If you want to hold the finished waffles until serving time, preheat your oven to 200°F.

❷ Melt the butter; reserve. In a large bowl, whisk together the flour, baking powder, baking soda, salt, zest, spices, and brown sugar (check that it's free of lumps when you add it). In another bowl, whisk together the milk, orange juice, and eggs until well combined. Add the vanilla and almond extracts and stir to mix. Pour the liquid ingredients over the dry ingredients and blend with the whisk. Stir in the plums and the melted butter.

❸ Lightly butter or spray the grids of your waffle iron, if needed. Brush or spray the grids again only if subsequent waffles stick.

❹ Spoon out a full ½ cup of batter (or the amount recommended by your waffler's manufacturer) onto the grids. Spread the batter evenly with a metal spatula or wooden spoon. Close the lid and bake until golden and set. Serve the waffles immediately or keep them, in a single layer, on a rack in the preheated oven while you make the rest of the batch.

Topping: Orange-Plum Sauce

This sauce has a beautifully balanced sweet-tart taste and is so remarkably good with ice cream that you might want to double the recipe so you'll have extra on hand.

2 sweet ripe plums (about ½ pound total)
1 cup fresh orange juice

¼ cup firmly packed light brown sugar

Pit the plums and cut them into small pieces. Place the plums, orange juice, and brown sugar in a nonreactive medium-size saucepan. Cover and cook over medium heat, stirring occasionally, until the plums are very soft, about 20 minutes. Puree the mixture in a food processor or blender. Don't worry about the skin; it will puree too and add extra color and flavor to the sauce. (The sauce can be made up to 3 days in advance, covered, and refrigerated, or packed airtight and frozen for 2 weeks.) Serve the Orange-Plum Sauce cold, at room temperature, or warm.

SERVING: If you're serving whipped cream, pour some sauce over each waffle, then top with a spoonful of cream. If you're serving ice cream, put a scoop of ice cream on top of each waffle, then spoon over the sauce. And if you're serving the sauce as the solo topping, just pour it on. These are delicious in any and every combination. Save leftover sauce for topping pancakes or other kinds of waffles (try it over the Crispy Cornmeal Waffles at breakfast, page 44).

Rhubarb Waffles

Rhubarb has a tart, refreshing, citrusy flavor that goes well with many other fruits and flavorings. Here, small pieces of rhubarb are caramelized in butter and sugar and folded into a fragrant batter to produce a very soft, slightly chewy waffle that is superb served with a cascade of sweetened strawberries. Since rhubarb's season is short—it shows up during the summer and then, occasionally, makes a brief appearance at the greengrocer's in February—I urge you to make these splendid waffles whenever you see rhubarb in the market.

PLAN AHEAD: **Make the Glistening Strawberries before you make the waffles; set aside until needed.**

The Waffles

½ pound rhubarb, leaves removed, broad end of stalks trimmed
3 tablespoons unsalted butter
2 tablespoons sugar
½ teaspoon lemon juice
1 cup all-purpose flour
1½ teaspoons double-acting baking powder
¼ teaspoon baking soda
⅓ cup sugar

1¼ cups milk
1 large egg
½ teaspoon pure vanilla extract
1 teaspoon Grand Marnier or other orange liqueur (optional)

Vanilla ice cream or lightly sweetened crème fraîche (optional)

MAKES ABOUT FIVE 6½-INCH ROUND WAFFLES

❶ Use a vegetable peeler to remove the top layer from the rhubarb stalks, just the way you'd peel a carrot. Wash, dry well, and cut the rhubarb crosswise into ¼-inch-thick slices. Melt the butter in a medium-size skillet, add the rhubarb, and cook over medium-low heat, stirring, until the fruit softens and starts to melt into a puree, about 5 minutes. Add the 2 tablespoons sugar, raise the heat to medium-high, and cook for 2 minutes more to caramelize. Remove the skillet from the heat and stir in the lemon juice; set aside.

❷ Preheat your waffle iron. Preheat the oven to 350°F so you can crisp the waffles after they are made.

❸ In a large bowl, whisk together the flour, baking powder, baking soda, and the ⅓ cup sugar. In another bowl, whisk together the milk and egg. Add the vanilla and Grand Marnier, if using it, and whisk to blend. Pour the liquid ingredients over the dry ingredients and whisk together until just combined. Stir in the reserved rhubarb.

❹ Lightly butter or spray the grids of your waffle iron, if needed. Brush or spray the grids again only if subsequent waffles stick.

❺ Spoon out ½ cup of batter (or the amount recommended by your waffler's manufacturer) onto the iron, spreading it evenly across the grids with a metal spatula or wooden spoon. Close the lid and bake until golden. This waffle can be very soft, and you may find it difficult to lift the finished waffle off the grid. Don't worry. Just peel it off the grid slowly and carefully with a fork and spatula and keep it on a cooling rack while you make the rest of the batch. To reheat and crisp, put the waffles, in a single layer, on a rack in the preheated oven.

Topping: Glistening Strawberries

This is a simple, lovely way to prepare strawberries for topping waffles, pound cake, or ice cream. They are sweet, shiny, and abundantly juicy. The combination of strawberries and orange is a classic, and one that best brings out the pleasantly puckery quality that distinguishes rhubarb.

1 quart ripe juicy strawberries	1 tablespoon Grand Marnier or
¼ to ½ cup sugar	other orange liqueur
⅓ cup fresh orange juice	(optional)

Brush away any little bits of soil or debris clinging to the berries, hull them, cut them into thin slices, and toss with ¼ cup sugar, the orange juice, and the Grand Marnier, if you're using it. Taste and add more sugar, if needed. Set aside, stirring now and then, while you make the waffles. (The berries can be prepared 2 to 3 hours ahead, covered, and refrigerated until needed.)

SERVING: Serve the waffles warm with a spoonful of glistening berries, pouring the strawberry "juice" across the waffles so the grids can catch it. If you want to, you can finish these with a scoop of ice cream or some very lightly sweetened crème fraîche. Any leftover berries can be pureed and used as a topping for other waffles, such as Plain-and-Easy Breakfast Quickies (page 37).

Chocolate-Amaretti Heartbreakers

These are really waffled cakes—moist, cocoa-rich, and flecked with ground amaretti (Italian macaroons) and bittersweet chocolate. They're delicious as is with just a sprinkling of confectioners' sugar, luscious with lightly sweetened, softly whipped cream, and downright indulgent with ice cream and Hot Fudge Sauce (page 95).

3 large double amaretti (or 6 amaretti from 3 paper-wrapped packets)
2 ounces high-quality bittersweet chocolate
5 tablespoons unsalted butter
1¼ cups all-purpose flour
1½ teaspoons double-acting baking powder
¼ teaspoon baking soda
Dash of salt
¾ cup sugar

⅓ cup cocoa, preferably Dutch-processed
1½ cups milk
1 teaspoon pure vanilla extract
¼ teaspoon pure almond extract
2 large eggs

Confectioners' sugar, sweetened whipped cream, ice cream, and/or Hot Fudge Sauce (optional)

MAKES ABOUT 10 FULL FIVE-OF-HEARTS OR ABOUT SIX
6½-INCH ROUND WAFFLES

❶ Place the amaretti and bittersweet chocolate in the workbowl of a food processor or a blender and process until pulverized; reserve.

❷ Preheat your waffle iron. If you'd like to serve these warm, preheat your oven to 350°F.

❸ Melt the butter; reserve. In a large bowl, whisk together the flour, baking powder, baking soda, salt, sugar, and cocoa. In another bowl, whisk together the milk, vanilla, almond extract, and eggs until well blended. Pour the liquid ingredients over the dry ingredients and stir with the whisk to combine. Fold in the reserved amaretti-chocolate mixture and the melted butter.

❹ Lightly butter or spray the grids of your waffle iron, if needed. Brush or spray the grids again only if subsequent waffles stick.

❺ Spoon out ⅓ cup of batter (or the amount recommended by your waffler's manufacturer) onto the hot iron, spreading it evenly with a metal spatula or wooden spoon. Close the lid and bake until just set. Bake these slightly less than you do other waffles because chocolate has a tendency to burn easily. There's no need to worry, but you do want to keep an eye on these. Transfer finished waffles to a cooling rack while you make the rest of the batch. Right before serving, warm these briefly, about 2 minutes, in the oven—or don't. They're good at room temperature, too.

SERVING: I like to present a full five-of-hearts to each person, shaking a dusting of confectioners' sugar over the entire waffle and then scooping some whipped cream or ice cream onto the center. Hot Fudge Sauce (page 95) is both luscious and luxurious over these. Broken into individual hearts and filled with ice cream, these make fabulous sandwiches (see the recipe for Gingerbread Ice-Cream Hearts, page 168, for directions on how to fill them).

Pumpkin Pie Waffles

These may never replace pumpkin pie at a traditional Thanksgiving dinner, but they'll give tradition a good race. They are comforting, custardy, and filling like pumpkin pie. I make them with the same spices I use for pumpkin pie and add sour cream for smoothness; the dark rum is there for extra flavor and a little mystery.

5 tablespoons unsalted butter
1 cup pumpkin puree (you can use canned puree)
½ cup firmly packed dark brown sugar
¼ cup granulated sugar
1¼ teaspoons ground cinnamon
1¼ teaspoons peeled grated fresh ginger
⅛ teaspoon ground cloves
⅛ teaspoon freshly grated nutmeg

Pinch of salt
1⅓ cups all-purpose flour
1 tablespoon double-acting baking powder
½ teaspoon baking soda
1 cup milk
½ cup sour cream
2 large eggs
2 tablespoons dark rum
1 teaspoon pure vanilla extract

Vanilla ice cream and/or maple syrup for accompaniments

MAKES ABOUT SIX 4½-INCH SQUARE BELGIAN WAFFLES

❶ Preheat your waffle iron. If you want to hold the finished waffles until serving time, preheat your oven to 200°F.

❷ Melt the butter; reserve. In a large bowl, combine the pumpkin, sugars, spices, and salt. Mix together well with a rubber spatula or small electric mixer. Stir in the flour, baking powder, and baking soda. The mixture will be thick and a little lumpy. Don't try to smooth it out; just mix until the ingredients are incorporated. In another bowl, beat together the milk, sour cream, eggs, rum, and vanilla. Add the liquid ingredients to the pumpkin mixture and stir until combined. Fold in the melted butter.

❸ Whether or not your iron's grids are well seasoned or made of a nonstick material, it is best to lightly butter or spray the grids for these waffles; the batter is quite sticky. Brush or spray the grids again only if subsequent waffles stick.

❹ Spoon out ⅔ to ¾ cup of batter for a Belgian waffler (or the amount recommended by your waffler's manufacturer) onto the iron, spreading it evenly with a metal spatula or wooden spoon. Close the lid and bake until golden. If the waffle is hard to remove from the iron, peel it off gently and carefully. Serve immediately or keep the waffles, in a single layer, on a rack in the preheated oven while you make the rest of the batch.

SERVING: Serve these warm and golden, one to a diner, with the toppings of your choice. They're great with a cup of hot or cold cider.

White Chocolate Chip Waffles

White chocolate is a chameleon: Depending on what you blend it with, it can taste like chocolate or vanilla. In these golden sweet waffles, white chocolate tastes definitively of vanilla. Here, white chocolate chips are blended with the tropical flavors of pure vanilla extract, shredded coconut, and dark rum. The mix is appealing, and the texture somewhat surprising, since the white chocolate chips melt and then firm as the waffle cools, providing unexpected crunch. Oddly enough, pouring ribbons of creamy Milk Chocolate–Rum Sauce over these waffles intensifies rather than diminishes their strong vanilla flavor.

PLAN AHEAD: **Prepare and refrigerate the Milk Chocolate–Rum Sauce before you start the waffles.**

The Waffles

5 tablespoons unsalted butter
1½ cups all-purpose flour
1 tablespoon double-acting
   baking powder
⅓ cup sugar
1½ cups milk
2 large eggs
1 teaspoon pure vanilla extract
1 tablespoon dark rum

½ cup shredded coconut,
   preferably unsweetened
   (available in health food
   stores)
½ cup white chocolate chips

Lightly sweetened whipped
   cream (optional)

MAKES ABOUT EIGHT 4½-INCH SQUARE BELGIAN WAFFLES

❶ Preheat your waffle iron. If you want to hold the finished waffles until serving time, preheat your oven to 200°F.

❷ Melt the butter; reserve. In a large bowl, whisk together the flour, baking powder, and sugar. In another bowl, whisk together the milk, eggs, vanilla, and rum until well blended. Pour the liquid ingredients over the dry ingredients and whisk until just combined. Fold in the coconut, chips, and melted butter.

❸ Lightly butter or spray the grids of your waffle iron, if needed. Brush or spray the grids again only if subsequent waffles stick.

❹ Spoon out 1 cup of batter for a Belgian waffler (or whatever measure is recommended by your waffler's manufacturer) onto the grids. Gently spread the batter across the grids with a metal spatula or wooden spoon. Close the lid and bake until golden and set. Serve the waffles immediately, or keep them, in a single layer, on a rack in the preheated oven while you make the rest of the batch.

Topping: Milk Chocolate–Rum Sauce

This milk chocolate sauce is smooth, satiny, and only slightly sweet, its mild flavor rounded with dark cocoa, rum, and vanilla. A small amount of corn syrup is mixed into the sauce, just enough to help give it the texture of a great hot fudge sauce—the kind that ribbons as it pours.

2 tablespoons firmly packed light brown sugar
1 tablespoon cocoa, preferably Dutch-processed
Dash of salt
2 tablespoons light corn syrup

¾ cup milk
3½ ounces milk chocolate, finely chopped
1 tablespoon unsalted butter
1 teaspoon dark rum
½ teaspoon pure vanilla extract

Whisk together the brown sugar, cocoa, salt, and corn syrup in a heavy-bottomed medium saucepan to blend. Still whisking, gradually add the milk. Bring the mixture to the boil over medium heat, stirring occasionally. Reduce the heat to medium-low and cook, stirring, for 3 minutes. Remove the pan from the heat and stir in the chocolate, stirring until the chocolate is melted and the mixture is smooth. Add the butter, rum, and vanilla and stir until blended. Pour the sauce into a clean jar or bowl, press a piece of plastic wrap against the surface, and refrigerate until needed. (The sauce can be made up to 1 week ahead, covered tightly, and refrigerated.)

SERVING: I'd suggest serving two square waffles to each person, pouring chocolate sauce over and around the waffles, and topping each waffle with a spoonful of whipped cream, as though you were making an ice cream sundae. The chocolate sauce is delicious warm or cold.

Triple Apple Waffles

Apples show up in three forms in this fabulous fall-becoming-winter dessert. Fresh apples are sautéed in butter and sugar until they are sweetly caramelized for the topping; full-bodied cider provides some of the liquid for the waffle batter; and spiced apple butter, the slow-cooked essence of apples, is added to the batter to give the waffles a profoundly apple-flavored tang. Together they create a completely satisfying, soft-textured, well-spiced dessert.

PLAN AHEAD: Make the waffles first and set them aside while you prepare the caramelized apple topping. Reheat just before serving.

The Waffles

3 tablespoons unsalted butter
1 cup all-purpose flour
2 teaspoons double-acting
  baking powder
½ teaspoon ground cinnamon
¼ teaspoon ground ginger
Pinch of freshly grated nutmeg
2 tablespoons firmly packed
  light brown sugar

2 tablespoons granulated sugar
½ cup apple cider
½ cup milk
2 large eggs
¼ teaspoon pure vanilla extract
¼ cup spiced apple butter

Vanilla ice cream or lightly
  sweetened whipped cream

MAKES ABOUT 6 FULL FIVE-OF-HEARTS WAFFLES

❶ Preheat your waffle iron. Preheat your oven to 350°F so you can reheat the waffles after they are made.

❷ Melt the butter; reserve. In a large bowl, whisk together the flour, baking powder, spices, and sugars. In another bowl, whisk together the cider, milk, eggs, and vanilla until well blended. Pour the liquid ingredients over the dry ingredients and stir well with the whisk. Mix in the apple butter and fold in the melted butter.

❸ Whether or not your iron's grids are well seasoned or made of a nonstick material, it is best to lightly butter or spray the grids of your iron for these waffles; the batter is quite sticky. Brush or spray the grids again only if subsequent waffles stick.

❹ Spoon out ½ cup of batter (or the amount recommended by your waffler's manufacturer) onto the hot grids. Spread the batter evenly with a metal spatula or wooden spoon. Close the lid and bake until browned and set. These waffles are best if you turn them over midway through their baking. Use a fork and a spatula to lift the soft waffle off the grids (these tend to be very soft, so you may find yourself peeling them off the iron), turn them over, close the iron, and continue baking until done. Keep the finished waffles on a cooling rack while you make the rest of the batch. Right before serving, reheat them, putting them in a single layer on a rack in the oven, for about 3 minutes.

Topping: Caramelized Apples

Sautéing apples in butter and sugar gives them a creamy butterscotch color that is a handsome contrast to the dark apple waffles. Serve the apples hot from the skillet to get their fullest flavor.

2 pounds (about 5 or 6) firm
  Golden Delicious apples
2 teaspoons fresh lemon juice
4 tablespoons (½ stick)
  unsalted butter

⅓ cup sugar
¼ cup apple cider
2 tablespoons dark rum
  (optional)

Peel, core, and halve the apples. Cut them crosswise into thin slices and place them in a bowl with the lemon juice. Toss to coat the slices with juice. Melt the butter in a large skillet over medium heat; add the sugar and stir until moistened. Add the apples and sauté, stirring constantly, until soft, brown, and lightly caramelized, about 10 minutes. Add the cider and bring to the boil. Add the rum, if using it, and cook another minute to boil off the alcohol. These are ready to serve, but they can wait in the skillet a few minutes while you reheat the waffles.

SERVING: I like to serve a whole five-of-hearts to each person, topping each waffle with caramelized apples in the center and a scoop of ice cream or whipped cream off to the side. Of course, you can separate the hearts and put a few on each plate or, if you've made the Triple Apple Waffles in a waffler of a different shape, you can cut the waffles into whatever sizes please you and serve the apples mounded in the center of the plate with the waffles around them.

Tiramisù Waffles

Made with mascarpone—a triple-cream Italian cheese—coffee, cinnamon, and small pieces of bittersweet chocolate, these waffles contain all the best flavors of a rich, tempting tiramisù. The waffles bake to a light brown and are soft and cakey, with an inner sponge that has the same meltaway creaminess as custard. Topped with a strongly flavored, chilled espresso sauce, these are irresistible whether served on their own or following a lavish dinner.

PLAN AHEAD: Make the Espresso Custard Sauce a few hours—or as many as 2 days—ahead so it has time to chill properly. The whipped cream can be made at serving time.

The Waffles

3 tablespoons unsalted butter	½ cup mascarpone
1 cup all-purpose flour	½ cup hot strong coffee
1 teaspoon double-acting baking powder	2 large eggs
¼ teaspoon baking soda	½ cup milk
1 teaspoon ground cinnamon	2 tablespoons dark rum
2 teaspoons instant espresso powder	2 ounces bittersweet chocolate, finely chopped

MAKES ABOUT SIX 6½-INCH ROUND WAFFLES

❶ Preheat your waffle iron. Preheat your oven to 350°F so you can reheat the waffles after they are made.

❷ Melt the butter; reserve. In a medium-size bowl, whisk together the flour, baking powder, baking soda, cinnamon, and espresso powder to combine. In a large bowl, beat the mascarpone until satiny; gradually beat in the hot coffee. The cheese will melt, but the mixture may not be entirely smooth—that's fine. One by one, add the eggs, milk, and rum, beating until well blended. Stir in the dry ingredients, chopped chocolate, and melted butter.

❸ Whether or not your iron's grids are well seasoned or made of a nonstick material, it is best to lightly butter or spray the grids of your iron for these waffles; the batter is quite sticky. Brush or spray the grids again only if subsequent waffles stick.

❹ Spoon out a generous ½ cup of batter (or the amount the waffler's manufacturer suggests) onto the grids. Use a metal spatula or wooden spoon to smooth the batter evenly over the grids. Close the lid and bake until the waffle is lightly browned on the underside, then carefully turn it over to brown on the other side. (You'll need to handle these gently; they're cakey and quite soft.) Put the finished waffles on a cooling rack while you make the rest of the batch. Just before serving, warm the waffles for about 3 minutes in the oven.

Topping: Espresso Custard Sauce

This custard sauce, powerfully flavored with espresso, is satiny smooth, only slightly thickened, and hardly sweet at all—the ideal companion for Tiramisù Waffles.

1 cup milk		2 teaspoons instant espresso
3 large eggs		powder
⅓ cup sugar		½ teaspoon pure vanilla extract

❶ Pour the milk into a heavy-bottomed, medium-size saucepan and bring to the boil. Meanwhile, in a medium-size bowl, beat the eggs and sugar together with a hand-held mixer or whisk until the mixture thickens and pales. Add the espresso powder and beat until combined.

❷ Very slowly pour a little of the hot milk into the bowl with the egg mixture, mixing all the while. Gradually add the rest of the milk, continuing to mix constantly. Pour the mixture back into the saucepan and cook over medium heat, stirring without stop with a wooden spoon, until the custard thickens slightly, about 2 minutes. The sauce is ready when you can run your finger down the length of the bowl of the wooden spoon and it doesn't fill in your track. Pour the sauce through a strainer into a clean bowl and stir in the vanilla. Cover with a piece of plastic wrap pressed against the surface; refrigerate until well chilled, about 3 hours. (You can make the sauce up to 2 days in advance; cover well and keep refrigerated until needed.)

continued

Garnish: Whipped Cream

This is a basic recipe for delicious, lightly sweetened whipped cream. Because the whipped cream will be piped into rosettes, it needs to be whipped until it is firmer than you'd want it to be were you just spooning it over a dessert. To avoid the risk of overwhipping, it is best to finish whipping the cream by hand, using a whisk to achieve just the consistency you want.

1 cup heavy cream
½ teaspoon pure vanilla extract

1 tablespoon confectioners' sugar

At serving time, use a mixer to whip the heavy cream with the vanilla and sugar just until it holds soft peaks. Switch to a whisk and beat until the cream holds firm peaks.

SERVING: Pour a small circle of chilled custard sauce onto the center of each dessert plate. It's nice to use large dinner-size plates for this presentation. Cut the waffles into quarters and arrange them in a circle, points toward the center. (You'll have the points of the wedges in the sauce, the rest of the waffle out of the sauce.) Now, decorate each waffle point with a rosette of whipped cream piped out of a tube with a star tip or a little dollop of cream dropped from a small spoon. Place the remainder of the cream in a bowl with a spoon and pass it at the table. (You might want to bring any remaining sauce along, also. The sauce is good enough to drink, and your guests might want a bit extra.)

Lemon Meringue Waffles

This dessert resembles a small lemon meringue pie. The base is a waffle that gets its tang from a triple dose of lemon—zest, juice, and extract. It is topped with rich lemon curd and swirls of meringue. You can make the waffles weeks ahead, have the filling ready in advance as well (or buy lemon curd from a specialty shop), and then, when you want to serve a dazzling dessert to special friends, just assemble the parts.

PLAN AHEAD: If you're going to make homemade Lemon Curd, you need to prepare it before you make the waffles. The Meringue should be prepared and baked just before you're ready to serve dessert.

The Waffles

4 tablespoons (½ stick) unsalted butter	Juice and grated zest of 3 lemons (separate the juice and zest)
1½ cups all-purpose flour	1 cup milk (approximately)
2 teaspoons double-acting baking powder	2 large eggs
¼ teaspoon baking soda	1 teaspoon pure lemon extract
½ cup sugar	

MAKES ABOUT 6 FULL FIVE-OF-HEARTS WAFFLES OR SIX
6½-INCH ROUND WAFFLES

❶ Preheat your waffle iron.

❷ Melt the butter; reserve. In a large bowl, whisk together the flour, baking powder, baking soda, and sugar. Pour the lemon juice into a glass measuring cup (you'll need one that holds at least 1 pint) and add enough milk to measure 1½ cups. If the measuring cup is large enough, add the eggs and the lemon extract and beat well; if not, pour the liquid into another bowl, add the eggs and lemon extract, and beat well. Pour the liquid ingredients over the dry ingredients and stir with the whisk until just combined. Stir in the grated lemon zest and melted butter.

❸ Lightly butter or spray the grids of your waffle iron, if needed. Brush or spray the grids again only if subsequent waffles stick.

continued

❹ Spoon out ½ to ⅔ cup of batter (or a little more than your waffler's manufacturer recommends) onto the grids. The batter needs a nudge, so use a metal spatula or wooden spoon to spread it evenly across the grids. Close the lid (you'll get a blast of fabulously fresh lemon scent as soon as the heat hits the batter) and bake until the underside is set; turn the waffle over and continue to bake until done. Remove the waffle from the iron. Keep the finished waffles on a cooling rack while you make the rest of the batch. If you've made the waffles early in the day, wrap them well and refrigerate until serving time.

Filling: Lemon Curd

Lemon curd is a rich, thickened custard, smoothed with butter and made puckery tart with lemon zest and juice. You can buy fine imported lemon curd by the jar in specialty shops, but homemade curd is both delicious and easy to make.

1¼ cups sugar
6 tablespoons unsalted butter,
   cut into 6 pieces

6 large egg yolks
1 large egg
Juice of 4 lemons

Put all the ingredients in a heavy-bottomed 2-quart saucepan and stir with a wooden spoon to moisten the sugar. Place over medium-low heat and cook, stirring constantly, until the butter melts and the mixture becomes custardy, about 4 to 6 minutes after the butter melts. Don't walk away; this can curdle. When the curd thickens slightly (it will thicken more as it cools) and you can run your finger along the length of the spoon's bowl without it filling in your track, pour the curd into a clean bowl or jar. Press a piece of plastic wrap against the surface and cool to room temperature. Refrigerate until needed, or up to 3 months.

Topping: Meringue

This is a featherweight topping of sweetened egg whites, beaten until they form stiff, glossy peaks, then browned in a hot oven. It is an extremely attractive finishing touch to a dessert and one that is simple to achieve.

6 large egg whites
⅛ teaspoon salt

¾ cup sugar

Right before you're ready to serve dessert, preheat your oven to 400°F. In a large, clean dry bowl with clean dry beaters, whip the egg whites and salt together until they form soft peaks. Slowly and gradually (a tablespoon or two at a time) add the sugar, beating all the while, and whip until the meringue holds firm peaks and has a satiny sheen.

FILLING AND BAKING: Place the waffles on a large baking sheet. Spread the Lemon Curd over the waffles, making an even circle of filling and leaving about a ½-inch circle uncovered around the outer edge of each waffle. Cover the curd with Meringue, making sure the meringue reaches all the way to the edge of each waffle. Use a small spoon or knife to swirl the meringue in an attractive pattern. Bake the waffles until the peaks of the meringue are browned, about 6 to 8 minutes. Remove from the oven and serve immediately.

SERVING: The prettiest way to serve this dessert is to offer each person a whole waffle circle, but if you think this may be too much, you can cut each portion down before you top the waffle with curd and meringue. I find the most attractive way to do this is to cut each circle into thirds; that way each portion will look like a wedge of pie.

Index

About the Author

Food writer Dorie Greenspan trained and worked as a pastry chef. She is the author of *Sweet Times: Simple Desserts for Every Occasion* (William Morrow, 1991), and editor-in-chief of *News from the Beard House,* the monthly food and wine magazine of The James Beard Foundation. Her recipes and articles have appeared in *The New York Times, Bon Appétit, Food & Wine,* and *Elle.* She lives in New York and Westbrook, Connecticut, with her husband, Michael, and their son, Joshua.